The Role of Military in Politics : A Case Study of Bangladesh

The Role of Military in Politics : A Case Study of Bangladesh

Charu Lata

Neha Publisher & Distributars
Delhi-110085

Publisher
Neha Publisher & Distributar
D-593, Sector-1 Rohini
Delhi-110085
Ph. 65763096, 9313574531

Distributed by
Gaurav Book Center
4832/24 Prahlad Gali
S-204 Ansari Road
New Delhi-2
Ph. 43570976, 9873096176

Edition : 2008

ISBN : 978-81-905415-7-2

Typing
Swati Computers
Delhi-110095
ph. 9868778438

Price : 725.00

Printed in India

Published by Mrs. S. Choudhary for Neha Publisher & Distributar, Delhi-85, Typeset by Manoj Kumar, Printed at Nag ri Printers, Delhi-32

Contents

PREFACE

This study is an explanatory attempt at analysing the role of military in politics of Bangladesh under the general pattern of the role of military in the politics of developing countries. In most of the developing countries military came to play an active role in political sphere when the democratic systems of these countries failed. In the particular case of Bangladesh like many other developing countries, the role of environmental factores as well as military establishment factors have been analysed.Several individuals and institutions rendered me great help during preparation of this work. My greatest thanks to Dr. Rajinder Singh Chauhan for the inspiration, encouragement and affection, which he gave me during the entire period of my study. Without his precious, steady and patient guidance, this work would not have been completed.

I am thankful to Dr. Gopal Singh and Dr. Javed Alam for providing me with their views and material for my work. I acknowledge my thanks to H.P. University for helping me financially by providing fellowship for my research on the same topic.

I wish to thank Ms. Jahan Ara Siddiqui, First Secretary and Mr. A.F.M. Nurus Safa Chowdhary, Second Secretary, of Bangladesh High Commission, New Delhi 1992 for providing me with the valuable information and material on Bangladesh. I am thankful to Ms. Veeni Kukrija and Mr. Gautam Basu whose writings and works inspired and helped me to a great extent.

My special thanks to the liberarians of Indian Council of World Affairs Library New Delhi; The Institute of Defence Studies and Analysis, New Delhi; India International Centre, New Delhi; National Archives Library, New Delhi; Delhi University Central Library, Delhi; Jawhar Lal Nehru University Library, New Delhi; Instutute of Advanced Study, Shimla; Subhash Chandra Institute Library, Calcutta; Bangalore University Central Library, Bangalore for allowing me to use their libraries for collection material for my research. I am thankful to their staff of Indian Council of World Affairs Library and Miss. Amrit Varsha Gandhi of National Archives Library, Who Provided me great help while collecting data.

I can not forget the co-operation extended to me by my friends, Manju and Meera during my work.

I thank my husband Kuldeep for providing me the moral support and for encouraging and helping me in finishing my work..

I am greatly thankful to my parents and family members, without whose understanding and encouragement. this work would not have been possible.

The only credit which I claim exclusively of mine is for the faults, which no reader will miss.

The book is an in-depth study on the various issues

involved in the politics of Bangladesh. The efforts have been made all through to find out what remains the basis as far as the functioning of military and politics is concerned. The polity of Bangladesh has been analysed through its establishment and through the independent years for restoration and development of democratic processes at the hands of changing military and civilian regimes.

In the backdrop of the contextuality of the problem, the role of military in politics in general and in Bangladesh in particular has been studied. This will help in understanding the discrenible pattern of civil-military relations, basis of military intervention in politics and reasons for the failure of democracy. In case of Bangladesh the impact of Bangladesh nationalist movement on the role of army in its politics is important to analyse. Other issues which are important to analyse are: the impact of modernisation on the role of army in the politics of Bangladesh, the impact of modernised army on the process of socio-economic transformations, the ideology perpetuated or ascended by military rulers, the strategies applied by military rulers for legitimising their rule, the causes for unsucessaful and successful coups and counter-coups and the specific nature of Bangladesh's military establishent which led it into the sphere of politics.

For the investigation of the issues posed above, the scientific study has focused on micro as well as macro analysis of the role of military in politics. In my view it is interaction, overlapping, interlocking and interdependence of various environmental, cultural and socio-economic forces of society in relation to political sphere are important for empirical investigation. Each specific society has a structure of its own by the type of culture and socio-economic set-ups having their own type of political systems. It also gives rise to various varibles to dominate over others which determine the role of military in the sphere of politics. These facts and variables can be ascertained by empirically establishing various conditions under different situations.

The study is based on theretical as well as empirical works of eminent scholars on the subject. Though it is impossible to be free from the value biases of the researcher but a sternous effort has been made to explicit the implicit values by formulating the scientific schemes of chapterisation.

The first Chapter 'Introduction' provides in overview of the topic, right from its inception various factors innolveed in the politics of Bangladesh, which shape up the polity of country around civil-military lelations and the importance of democracy have been discussed.

The next chapter, 'Theoretical Questions' deals with the review of existing theories on the role of military in politics in general and in Bangladesh in particular. The hypothesis and inferences have also been drawn after critical evaluation of the available literature. This is necessary for our investigation of the problem. Construction of theory is important for explaining and defining the concept. The working definition can be obtained and a definite course can be chartered out only after proving the theoretical questions. Theoretical questions will help cummulatively in micro as well as macro analysis.

The third chapter 'Historical Background' analyses the ideological and cultural foundation of the nationalist movement and the role of armed bands in nationalist liberation movement which assumed language question from 1948-

54, federal balance and regional autonomy from 1954-65 and national liberation movement from 1965-71. This chapter also deals with formation of social forces such as military, armed bands and political resistence movements which emerged in the liberation struggle of Bangladesh. The chapter also tries to get to the roots of the relations between civilian society and armed bands and also military and armed bands in historical perspective. Histoicity of the problem is important for fourmulating analytical freamework for the understanding of political phenomenon. Because men, groups, nations do not act only as they want to, but are also conditioned by historical circumstances.

"Army and Political Institutions" explains the nature and characteristics of political institutions i.e., executives, legislatives, jidiciary, parliament, political parties, pressure groups bureaucracy etc., and their relations with army. The chapter also takes into account the level of political culture.

The army rule does not operate in vacuum, it is a product of definite socio-economic set up. Therefore, the next chapter, 'Army and socio-economic modernisation' deals with the level of socio-economic development of Bangladesh society and the level of modernisation of Bangladesh army. It also analyses the role of army as an instrument of socio-economic modernisation and impact of modernisation on the nature of military organisation.

The last chapter, 'Military establishment' tries to explore the military establishment variables such as ideology, recruitment, training, social composition and representativeness, level of factionalism, level of professionalisation, level of factionalism, level of techincal know-how etc., as the basis for fascilitating or retarding the role of military in the politics of Bangladesh. The chapter explains the very nature of military establishment in Bangladesh. It evaluates the role of civil-military relations, including the causes for coups and counter coups, the military's espousing cause for promoting the popular rule and the natures of conflict. While external factors like political institutions and socio-economic changes act merely as catalytic agents, the bases of involment of military into the political spheres lie within itself.

All the chapters cover the media's role in various areas and in various form amidst the ongoing process of socio-economic and political chenges, which are disectly selated to the role of military in general and to the case of Bangladesh in particular.

The conclusions and the finding have been summarised at the end by drawing a picture of generalisations explaining the nature and direction to the politics and military in Bangladesh.

The secondary sources include the published material, such as books, articles, research journals, autobiographies, magazines and published material in news papers, which are concerned with to the role of military in general and in particular in Bangladesh. The military's espousing cause for promoting the popular rule and the natures of conflict. While external factors like political institutions and socio-economic changes act merely as catalytic agents, the bases of involment of military into the political spheres have direct effect on media and its role.

Charu Lata

I-Introduction

The current era of democratic transitions constitutes the waves of democratisation in the history of the modern world.

"The first long wave of demoratisation began in 1820's with the widening of the suffrage to a large proportion of male population in the United States and continued for almost a century until 1926, bringing into being some twenty nine democracies. In 1922, however, the coming to power of Mussolini in Italy marked the beginning of a first reverse wave that by 1942 had reduced the number of democratic states in the world to twelve. The triumph of the allies in World War-II initiated a second wave of democratisation that reached its zenith in 1962 with thirty six countries being governed democratically, only to be followed by a second reverse wave (1960-1975) that brought the number of democracies back down to thirty[1]."

The causes that give rise to these shifting waves of democratisation and / or militarisation are of great academic interest and need to be enquired into by making objective as well as subjective study of the phenomenon.

1. Samuel P. Huntington, "Democracys' Thirs Wave," Journal of Democracy, Vol. II, No. 2, Spring, 1991, pp. 12-13.

"Nearly a sixth of humanity-about 800 million people live under military rule, more than one third of all nations, nearly half of the developing world and virtually the entire continents of South America and Africa and also important segments of Asia are goverened not by the rule of law but by the rule of bayonet[2]."

The concepts of democracy and legitimacy are interwined with the concepts of modernisation and political development. The first development of political modernisation was the consolidation of modern nation-states to which armies contributed a lot.

Military institutions came to occupy an increasingly important place in the societies of twentieth century as the character of warfare changed. "Twentieth century methods of warfare brought a reintegration of civilian and military instituions. The process of industrial mobilisation involved the redirection of civilian insitutions to military purposes and the reorientation of the military to make them able to utilise the machinery of industrial production[3]."

The importance of military instutitions has always been enhanced by periods of warfare. The occurance of two world wars within a period of twenty five years and series of military operations kept military leadership and organisation more or less constantly to the fore. Under the circumstances military became well planned and co-ordinated organisation. It, thus, became the most potent force making for comprehensive large scale organisation.

---

2. P.K.S. Namboodiri, "Bangladesh : Omnious Shadow of the Military," Strategic Analysis, Vol. VI, No. 5, August 1982, p. 277.

3. Carolin F Ware, K.M. Pannikar and J. M. Romein, History of Mankind : Cultural and Scientific Development. (London :

Although the military institutions in the twentieth century were usually conservative, with strong traditions which dedicated to the maintenance of the status-quo. But the modern military is both preserver and powerful innovators of social change. "The Soviet Red army after 1917 and the people's liberation army of China were direct instruments of revolution and reconstruction. The military provided much of the leadership from revolution and did modernisation in countries of the Middle-east e.g. Turkey, Iran and Eqypt. In some of the industrially underdeveloped countries such as Thailand, after the second world war, the armed forces were one of the agencies through which modern technology reached into a country.[4]"

In th early years of the century the military establishments of most countries had many common characteristics although the detail of their form and their role in national life varied considerably from place to place. "The German army from the time of its victory over the French in 1870 to the opening of the first world war, provided a model, or atleast an inspiration, to the professional military group in most other countries very notably in Turkey and Japan.[5]"

"All the countries of continental Europe and also Japan, had conscript armies composed of a permanent officer group, a nucleus of army regulars, chiefly non-commissioned officers and a large reserve of manpower which had experienced military training, usually for two years.[6]"

---

4. Ibid.
5. Ibid. p. 829
6. Ibid.

In case of emergency the volunteer armies were also the rule.

There was sharp cleavage between officers and men. officers generally came from the upper strata of the society and their career was viewed as one of great respect. In many countries such officers came from the special social group of large landowners a heritage from feudal society in which the two functions of landowing and fighting were combined. As the officers were drawn from the upper social strata, they dominated their sphere of activity and thus developed an authoritarian tendency in the military establishments.

In the liberal democracies military was subject to civilian control of funds and determination of policy. But, it had complete authority to take military decisions. "The military establishments in early years of the century were primarily concerned with men and only secondarily with equipments. Almost completely lacking in knowledge or experience of scientific or industrial methods, the military left the initiative in weapon production to private or public industry. While the military establishments themselves clung to an essentially feudalagarian out look, the weapon makers transformed the nature of warfare and ultimately, the nature and role of the military itself.[7]"

The changes in the warfare brought changes in the military establishment, mainly after first world-war. The linkages of military establishment to the feudal norms became a thing of past. the new character of warfare also changed the relationship among several military services. Armies and Navies came under different commands. The rise of air power introduced a third service.

The military establishments took on many of great

industrial enterprises. Modern business methods, office organisation, systems of record keeping, the use of communication equipments and all the paraphernalia for carrying on large scale industrial operations gave military institutions many of the characteristics of the civilian counterparts.

The second world war completed the transformation of the military establishments into central institutions of industrial socienties sharing and often leading in technical and scientific development. As the warfare became an intense contest for scientific advance, the military establishments added to themselves great scientific bodies engaged not only in applied but also in basic research. In the field of military production, the role of military establishments continued to expand until they became inextricably interwoven with the civilian economy.

The military participated actively in many civilian roles. They filled political, diplomatic and administrative posts. High officers frequently headed business enterprises when they retired from active service, casting their shadows into civilian life by way of the special position enjoyed by them.

The role of military in freedom struggle of developing countrles added new dimensions, military has been linked to the revical of nationalistic ideals i.e. the military working for the liberation of the national territory or for the overthrow or retaining of the social order. The military service, has functioned as an essential contributor for changing, the developing or political institutions.

---

7. Ibid. p. 843

In the developing nations, the 'nation-states' were "given" by colonial masters to the old societies of Asia, Africa and Latin America. All these nations were actually composition of various sub-nationalities temporarily brought together by the colonial powers for the ease of administration. Under the long history of colonial rule and opperssion most of the new nations were left with, "a heritage full of well entrenched feudal classes, an underdeveloped capitalist class with close links with the metropolitan bourgeoisie. The imperialist rule had also promoted national strife, caste conflicts, linguistic and religious clashes and econmic disparities between classes and between regions. The uneven economic development led to social, political and economic tensions and conflicts."[8]

After the new nations got independence, they started imitating the wesern model of modernisation and political development blindly, in order to catch up the social, political and economic level of developed societies of west. To achieve the economic and political aspirations the colonial leaders abruptly started transformation of their traditional social and economic orders. The western education, urbanisation, economic oppurtunities etc., enhanced social mobility, resulting in total restructuring of social values, affecting the traditional hereditary systems of authority. The unistitutionalised modernisation in the new nations gave rise to political crises and developed fissiparous tendencies which created instability, anarchy and chaos. Most of the new nations lacked, complex, co

---

8. Kalim Bahadur, V.D. Chopra and P.N. Huskar (eds) South Asia in Transition : Conflicts and Tensions, (New Delhi : Patriot Publishers, 1986), p. 7.

ordinated, specialised institutions; a highly productive economic system; modern transport and communication systems; wide-spread educational opportunities and a high level of literacy; social integration; and political institutions and processes that are capable of making and enforcing public policies. Under the institutional vacuum military acquired the strong incentives to move into the political sphere of these new nations.

The process of modernisation which started earlier in the developed world than it did in the developing world, differentiated the politics of developed world from that of the developing world. The countries of the developing world were "given states" prior to becoming nations. The most vital difference in the politics of developed and developing or under developed nations was the fact that "all change and development in the history of the developed world came about by consequence of commercialisation or, as a result of political, economic or religious conflicts within these societies, that were resolved by the play of indigenous forces and a minium of external intervention. Nationalism, statehood, in fact all change in the traditional colonised societies, on the other hand, were the crystallisation not of internal conflict and change but of the interction of the exogenous (colonial) forces with the indegenous."[9] Thus in the capitalist world there occured a natural transformation from feudalism to a form where occured a natural transformation from feudalism to a form

9. Edward Shils, "On the Comparative Study of the New States," inclifford Geertz (ed.) Old Societies and New Nations : The quest for Modernity in Asia and Africa, (New Delhi : Amerind Publications, 1963), p. 21.

where private ownership of instruments and means of production predominated. The change took place not as a result of invasion of foreign conquest but through the general disintegration of agricultural societies.

The developed societies were typified by bridging of the elite mass gap, the creation of a 'minium value' consensus, the devising of integrative institutions of behavior and a sense of territorial nategrative."[10] The armies in these societies came to be dominated by the civil authorities. The military servics was the hall mark of citizenship and citizenship the hall mark of political democracy.

The social origins and social mould of military with its upper class sense of guardianship of the state, worked in the United States and Great Britain on balance, to serve the process of internal parliamentary government. Armies played effective role in producing unified and homogenous societies in west.

Whereas, in the developing nations, the situation was altogether different. Colonialism had changed but by no means transformed the traditional social structures of the colonies. These societies had been given a veneer of modernisation but the efforts failed as the developing world presented the picture of dynasty, kingship and religious community as the principle of organisation. Legitimacy continued to be based on theocracy, noble birth or caste, religion and politics were inseparable and continued as before. So, the vision of modernisation of developing countries by adopting political institutions of west

---

10. Myron Weiner, 'Political Integration and Political Development,' in "The annals of the American Academy of Political Science." Vol. CCCLVIII 1965, p. 52-64.

faded soon and it became clear that these new symbols of modernity were clashing head on with the centuries old established structures of authority and organisation.

"In the crisis of modernisation, as in identity, legitimacy, penetration, participation, integration and distribution, the modernsning elite took resort to the formidable apparatus of state at their disposal, to stem the rising tide of threats to the very existence of the new nations."[11] These developing societies had very low economic productivity and high degree of social cleavages, so there was political gap between rulers and the ruled, economic gap between classes and social and cultural gaps between linguistic, racial or ethnic groups. Thus "the politics of these societies were fragile, unstable and porous. A tensions rose, the military appeared to be an effective source of stability when other elites lost legitimacy"[12]

Almost all the states of South, South-East Asia and Africa casted off the yoke of colonialism, adopted democratic constitutional systems for speedy developments under the democratic norms, the franchise was widely extended, political parties sprang into being and general elections determined the fate of the governments. The affirmations of devotion to democratic principles by the nationalist leaders were repealed and continuous."[13]

---

11. Lucian Pye, Aspects of Political Development (Boston : Little Brown and co., 1966), pp. 63-66.

12. Henry Bienen, The Military Intervenes : Case Studies in Political Development. (New York : Russell Sage Foundation, 1968), p. XV.

13. Rupert Emerson, From Empire to Nation. (Boston : Beacon Press, 1963), p. 227.

Although, most of the developing nations started with the commitment to follow the democratic forms of government, yet, within their very diest decades as independent sovereign states, it became clear that under the facade of republican character, their real systems were nearly everywhere authoritarian. "Even in nations traditionally idenfitied with the western values of democracy and libertarianism, parliamentary norms were more formal than real, with a single party and its dynamic leaders retaining a virtual monopoly of the political apparatus."[14]

Of the many democracies which emerged in the past century, only a handful have survived. Before long most of them have, lost their way and settled back into authoritarian of dictatorial regimes through coups and military revolts. "In nineteen fiftees, Pakistan, Burma and Sudan surrendered their civilian rule into the hands of military. In middle-east the revolution in Iraq installed a General in power and Lebanon elected the chief of its army to presidency."[15] In the mid sixties there was rash of military coups in Ghana, Leopoldville, Congo, the Central African Republic, Upper Volta and Nigeria, adding to those which had taken place in Algeria, Tago, Sudan and Braazaville Congo. This conclusively ended hopes that Africa would avoid going the way of Latin America, the middle-east, South and South-East Asia."[16] In Asia between 1958-74, There occured forty military interventions in different

---

14. Irwing Louis Horwitz, Three Worlds of Development (New York : Oxford University Press, 1972), pp. 27-29.

15. Rupert Emerson, op. cit.. pp. 276-77.

16. Samuel P. Huntington, Political Order in Changing Societies, (New Haven : Yale University Press, 1968), p. 192.

countries. In Africa there were fifty such interventions in different countries during the same period, while in Latin America there were thirty military interventions during 1958-74."[17] In 1989, There were over fifty developing countries which were dominated by armed forces."[18]

"One interesting similarity among forty odd muslim states in the world is that in spite of a wide variety and heterogeneity in terms of language, food, dress, etc. they are either urled by military men or by strong men supported by the military. Military is a great reality in the muslim states and civilian governments have existed either with the support of the military of may be if it is indifferent or neutral but never in opposition to it."[19]

An overall view of the muslim states shows that soldiers have governed a majority of the Middle Eastern (muslim) Between 1930 and 1960, the military over turned governments in muslim states on thirty occasions, and on several more, military pressure or support proved decisive in changing the composition or direction of government. In 1962 the army ruled six of the eighteen muslim states and constituted the main prop in another eight. In 1980, half of the muslim states were directly ruled by the mulitary, in the rest military was the ultimate power."[20]

---

17. Samuel E. Finer, The Man on the Horseback : The Role of Military in politics. (Harmondsworth : Penguin Books, 1975), pp. 272-73.

18. The Statesman, 20 November, 1989.

19. K.L. Kamal, "The Non-Military Activities of the Pakistan Military," South Asian Studies, Vol XVII, No. 1, Jan-June, 1982, p. 26.

20. Saleem Quereshi, "Military in the polity of Islam : Religion as a basis for Civil-Military Interacton," International Political Sci-

ence Review, Vol. II, No. 3, 1981, p. 271.

Military has its prevasive role even in some affluent countries like Greece, Turkey, South Korea and Taiwan. In Socialist China also, military injoys as much power as the party. The South Asian sub-contient is the important area in the world. But due to some negative developments the continent has not received that momentum of development that has taken place in the several regions of the world. South Asian countries : India, Pakistan, Bangladesh, Nepal, Bhutanm Srilanka, Maldives came into being when Britishers withdrew from the sub-contient. Almost all the countries opted for democracy but, democracy is still in the phase of transition in this sub-contient because of frequent military interventions. The British Indian Army, which is in fact the predecessor of the armed forces in all the South Asian States was trained from its very to promoting imperial interests. This politicised army to a greater extent. Even after independece military appeared frequently in these countries under crumbling law and order situations. Military has been active in political spheres of Srilanka and Maldives. Nepal is undergoing its experiments with democracy. Pakistan has had frequent military interventions.

Bangladesh being a component of South Asian region is having transitional military and democratic phases in its polity. In Bangladesh, military, first came into power in August, 1975, replaced the civilian regime and continued to rule under Gen. Zia-ur-Rahman until he was assassinated in May 1981. After Zia, a civilian politician Justice Abdus Sattar, the then vice president of the country succeeded. But this constitutional succession lasted only for a few months and armed forces took over. This time it was Gen. Ershad who turned the table on civilian rulers. After the nine year dictatorial regime of Ershad, civilian rule under Begam Khalida Zia succeeded.

The politics of Bangladesh has a direct impact on Indian Politics. It is important for India, for maintaining balance of power in South Asia against the countries like China. "After Pakistn, Bangladesh has been the second most important security liablity for India amongst South Asian neighbours untill now...Bangladesh occupies a strategic position over the Bay of Bengal...The vulnerablity of Bangladesh towards falling into the lap of any external power arises from the fact that there is abject poverty and under-development in one of the densely populated countries of the world. Therefore, the old rumours that Bangladesh may concede Chittagong and St. Martin's island as bases or facility points to the U.S. will have to be taken seriously. Bangladesh has also been improving its ties with China and Nepal. The Chinese interest in Bangladesh and especially the supply of armaments may acquire troublesome dimension for India."[21] "Bangladesh's graphical existence constitutes a weak point in Indian security in the strategic north-east regions."[22] Therefore, a democratic, secular and stable Bangladesh would be an asset to India.

---

21. Parminder S. Bhopal, "India's Security Environment in the 1990's : The South Asia Factor, "Strategic Analyses." Vol. XII, No. 7, Oct., 1989, p. 744.

22. Christopher H. Bateman, "National Security and Nationalism in Bangladesh," Asian Survey Vol. XIX, No. 8, August 1979, p. 783.

Bangladesh is one of the 'Crisis Regimes' as called by Amos Parlmutter."[23] of the new states in which there have been military interventions. "Between 1975 and 1991, there were about twenty copus and counter-coups whether successful or unsuccessful."[24] Bangladesh came into existence only in 1971, after the division of Pakistan. "Pakistan as it was found was the country unique in the world. It was divided into two wings separated by more than a thousand miles of hostile Indian territory and, also separated by distinct cultural and regional identities."[25] The total area of these two wings was 365,529 square miles, which was divided into two unequal regions : East Pakistan, 55,126 square miles and West Pakistan 360,403 square miles."[26] flanking the eastern and western borders of India.

For thirty years since the formation of Pakistan as a sovereign independent state, the military had been used very frequently to put down the volatile Bengali protesters in East against the policies of the arrogant Punjabi, Mujahir Pathan ruling elite of West. The democracy in the country had come to an end. Pakistan remained either under Martial law or controlled democracy after 1958.

---

23. Amos Permutter, 'The Comparative Analyses of Military Regimes : Formations, Aspirations and Achievements' "World Politics" Vol. XXXIII, No.1, October 1980, p. 313..

24. David Bergman, "Bangladesh's Opening for a New Beginning", Economic and Political weekly, Vol. XXVI, No. 7, Feb. 16, 1991, p. 729.

25. Taya Zinkin, "A Cooler look at Pakistan," 'Asian Review' Vol.1, No. 3 April, 1968, p. 248.

26. Rannaq Jahan, Pakistan : Failure in National Integration, (New York : Columbia University Press, 1972), p. 10.

"Demographically, Pakistan was composed of a number of distinct ethnic groups, although from beginning its leaders highlighted the strength of Islamic unity which recognised no regional, ethnic or linguistic loyalities. It was this fragile basis of religion that had created Pakistan in the first place as an artificial entity with no solid nation basis, carved out of muslim majority provinces of British India, With the two nation theory."[27] Pakistan was separated on the basis of Islam. Yet, when Pakistan came in existence, it became apparent that this was "an uneasy amalgam of distinct cultural, linguistic and ethnic groups."[28]

From 1948 to 1971, Bangladesh nation question in Pakistan assumed various dimensions. From 1948 to 1955 the language issue, from 1955 to 1968 disparity and federal question from 1968 to 1971, the Bangladesh national question assumed the seccessionist dimension.

The collision of nationalisms in 1947 and 1971 eventually drew the masses into the nationalist movement. The partition of India in 1947 was accompanied by large scale bloody riots in which minorities on either side of the new borders were comprehensively massacred, leading to large scale transfers of population. The emergence of Bangladesh in 1971 stemmed from a genocidal onslought by the Pakistani army against the Bengali masses, which resulted in an international war between India and Pakistan. "This led to estimates of over a million dead, million

---

27. Abha Dixit, "Ethnic and Regional Tensions in Pakistan," 'Strategic Analysis' Vol. XII, No. 12, p. 1458.

28. Ibid.

refugees seeking shelter in India leaving 90,000 Pakistani prisoners of war."[29]

"Lightning, it is said, does not strike the same spot a second time. Nor should colonialism, one would like to presume, hit the same country twice within the span of 200 years. For the victim is incapable experience and the moral and material strain involved. Yet, there seem to be a family resemblence between the methods employed, in East Bengal by the British imperialists in the nineteenth century and the West Pakistani colonialism imposed on the same country in the later decades of the twentieth. Indeed, in the scale of its brutality and its remorselessness, the pakistani variety, particularly in its later phase, beat the ways of the East India Company."[30]

Due to severe atrocities on East Pakistanis the open hostilitites between India and Pakistan were declared, the Indian troops moved in on 4 December, 1971, the support of the people for advancing troops was beyond all expectations. The masses rose as a body against the Pakistanis and supported the advancing troops with information, labour and transport at the risk of their lives. They shadowed the Pakistani actitivities closely and gave upto date and useful information about their man power, dispositions, mine layout and movement. Indian army played a great role in the liberation of Bangladesh. Addressing In-

---

29. Rehman Sobhan, "Political Dimentions of South Asian cooperation: The Perspective for Bangladesh." "Bids Research Report, Dhaka, No. 5, June, 1988, p. 9.

30. D.R. Mankekar, Pak-Colonialism in East Bengal, Ex-Colonial Turns Colonist. (New Delhi : Somaiya Publications Pvt. Ltd., 1971), p. 10.

dian troops at a farewell parade of Indian troops in Dacca after Bangladesh became independent, Mujib said, "You have sided with us in our peril. You trained our boys, gave them arms and joined in our struggle. I have no language to express my gratitude."[31]

Apart from Indian army, Mukti Bahini, the armed wing of Awami League, which included members of disbanded East Pakistan Rifles took part in liberation war and were taken in Pakistan army after liberation. Later on some of the armyamen loyal to Pakistan, Who hailed from Bangladesh were repatriated and regularised in Bangladesh army services. Many other armed wings also actively participated in liberation war. So the new regime number of loosely knit factions which managed to keep their cadress armed. These armed partisans posed a serious threat to the new government in its bid to impose its authority. Indiscriminate arming continued to pose a threat.

Bangladesh proclaimed its independence on December 16, 1971 and emerged to constitute the third component nation derived is said to be composed of two words 'Banga' and 'al' Benga was the name of the tribe and 'al' means bound. This is the bund that not merely froms the raised boundary between two pieces of cultivated land but also the mud-dyke that protects the land from floods-a common feature of a country full of rivers that constantly change course, and a heavy monsoon."[32]

---

31. Quoted in Maj. Gen. Lachman Singh, Victory in Bangladesh, (Dehradun : Natraj Publishers, 1981). p. 79.

32. Subrata Banerjee, Bangladesh (New Delhi : National Book Trust, 1981), p. 12.

Bangladesh has 108 million of population with annual growth rate (1981-91) 2.177% and density 750 per sq. km.[33] It is also worlds most densely populated country.[34] Already the country is as crowded as the United States of America would be if that continental country contained all the people on earth.[35] Population projections suggest that Bangladesh may have 157 million people by 2000. Population growth and its relationship to food production is therefore one of the most important problems of Bangladesh.[36]

The Bengali nation suddenly acquired responsibilities of self government. Democracy was thus a high risk for this new impoverished and second most populous of the 42 muslim nations.[37] The new state of Bangladesh occupied 55,598 sq. miles of territory, most of it surrounded by Indian. With the small area of 55, 598 sq. miles, Bangladesh is somewhat larger than that of England and

---

33. 'Staistical Pocket Book of Bangladesh' (Dacca : Bangladesh Bureau of Statistics, Ministry of Planning, Government of People's Republic of Bangladesh, 1992) p. 3.

34. M. Rashiduzzaman "East-West Conflicts in Pakistan : Bengali Regionalism in 1947-70" in Wilson, A. Jayaratnam and Dennis Dalton (eds). The States of South Asia : Problems of National Integration (Delhi : Vikas Publishing House Pvt. Ltd., 1982). p. 265.

35. Ibid.

36. World Development Report (London : Oxford University Press, 1991) Table 6., p. 184.

37. Charles Peter o'Donnell : Bangladesh : Biography of a muslim Nation (London : Westview Press, 1984), p. 1.

about the size of the U.S. states of Illinois or Wisconsin. It is larger than the state of Louisian, but much of Bangladesh's terrain resembles Louisiana's delta region. Among the nations of the world Bangladesh ranks with the smaller states of Eastern Europe but has a greater area than many West African and Central American nations."[38]

Geographically, Bangladesh is an eastern part of Bengal which is one of the largest delta in the world. It forms the major part of this delta having 87% of the total area in alluvial plains.[39]

"Bangladesh has 4000 km. border and is surrounded by Indian territory on the west, north and east and by the Bay of Bengal on the south. In the southern region however, near Chittagong and Cox's Bazar, it has a common boundary with Burma, the tract on either side of the Bangladesh and Burma boundary is mountainous and a road links Chittagong with Akyab in Burma, the plains of West Bengal are on the west, the Meghalya Plateau on the north and the Lushai and Mizo hills on the East. The drain of the country is from north to south and the major rivers flow in this direction into the Bay of Bengal. The whole terrain is plain except certain hilly areas in the east near Sylhat, Comilla and Chittagong. The Khulana area abounds in deltas and marshes.[40] Bangladesh is divided by the Ganga (Padma), Jamuna (Brahmaputra) and Meghna rivers.

---

38. Ibid. p.5.

39. Ranglal Sen, Political Elites in Bangladesh (New Delhi : K.P. Bhagchand andco., 1987). p. 7.

40. Maj. Gen Lachman Singh, op.cit. p. 2.

Bangladesh is a littoral state with nealy 41 400 miles of cost line.[41] The shore line of Bangladesh along the Bay of Bengal extends 370 miles from a western projection of Burma to the becaches of west Bengal. Fingers of Land intermingle with islands of varying sizes which strech along the coast formed by the three converging rivers as they empty into the Bay of Bengal. One of the extraordinary forests of the world nestles in the south west corner of the country, the Sunderban, a densely wooded tidal area of 2000 sq. miles, reaching from the main river branch of the delta to the Indian border near Calcutta, is a network of inland islands.[42]

Bangladesh has an agriculture oriented economy. The resource endowments of Bangladesh which principally determine economic potential are characterised by fertile soil, an abundance of forest resources, water resources and fish resources, rich deposits of limestone and considerable reserves of natural gas. The potential labour force is large, however the quality of labour force is low because of lack of education, particularly scientific and technical education, health and better medical and housing facilities which have not been provided even by the military rulers of the state.

The chances for the development of the agricultural sector in Bangladesh are fairly high. The land is extremely fertile. "The agriculture contributes more than sixty percent of the gross domestic product, employing about sev

---

41. Michael Brzoska and Thomad Charlson, Arms Transfer to the Third World 1971-85 (Oxford University Press, 1987). pp. 148-49.

42. Charles Peter o'Donnell op.cit. p.6

enty six percent of the total labour force and supporting 85 percent of total population. It is the base for 90% of the exports."[43] However, the growth of economy particularly in agriculture remains stagnant. The fact is that agriculture has been suffering from out dated feudal and semi-feudal production relations. "A handful of big farmers are owning big chunks of land. Indeed, the concentration of holding in few hands is still increasing giving rise to land-less labour. The middle and large farmers constitute less than fifteen percent of people but own almost fifty one percent of the land."[44]

Bangladesh possesses a comparative advantage in the production of rice and jute. It also has suitable conditions for tobacco and tea plantations. Among crops, rice domenates in terms of area and output, and is followed in value terms by based on agricultural raw material, forestry, fisheries, h ides and skin, limestone, n atural gas, jute, tabacoo, paper, textile etc. Fishing is a significant secondary occupation. Country boats and steamers are important means of communication. Life in Bangladesh depends on the proper planning of river system. Expect for jute, paddy and fishing, Bangladesh lacks commercial crops, which in term inhibit social change.

Bangladesh is predominatly rural, composed of approximately 68,000 villages in which the majority of popu-

---

43. S.R. Chakravarty, "Bangladesh : Survery of Domestic Scene" 'South Asian Studies' Vol. XII, No. 1 & 2, Jan-July, 1977, pp. 62-63.

44. Talukdar Maniruzzaman, Group Interests and Political Changes : Studies of Pakistan and Bangladesh (New Delhi : South Asian Publishers, 1982), p. 222.

lation lives.[45] Almost 95% of the total population is residing in rural areas.[46] The rural communities exist within a deltaic environment having pre-industrial technological conditions. The social basis of community organisation is homestead based patrilineal kin group. The village, thus, comprises homestead clusters, each cluster with a particular lineage. And the members of the dominent lineage exercise social influence and political power cover the community as a whole. The influentials from these lineages are known as matobbor[47] (headmen / spokesmen). The members of the village belong to a Somaj (little community). Somaj is extensive in character and different from kin groups. The village is an administrative political unit. The social organisations combine community atructure and class structures. The matabbor combines the doinance of property relations in social life and the dominant role of authority in the village. This points to the transformation of the functional power of a social minority into an exploitative power and domination by an exploitative class.

In fact, Bangladesh started with certain advantages which many of the new nations acutely lacked. First, culturally and linguistically, Bangladesh is the most homog

---

45. Ahmed Shafiql Huque, "Politics and Administration in a Periurban Country in Bangladesh." 'Asian Survey,' Vol. XXVI, No. 9. September, 1986. p. 959.

46. I.N. Mukherjee, "Economic Problems and Problems and Prospects of Bangladesh." 'International Studies.' vol. XIII, 1974, p. 278.

47. Hamza Alvi, "The State in Post Colonial Societies : Pakistan and Bangladesh." in K. Gough and H.P. Sharma (eds.), Monthly Review Press, 1973, p. 161.

enous of the states of South Asia. India, Pakistan and Srilanka are all culturally diverse. Almost whole of the population of Bangladesh speak one language i.e. Bengali, but, there are sharp economic cleavages. Only about two hundred families controlled the economy of Bangladesh. West Pakistan industrialists migrated to west Pakistan just before the emergence of Bangladesh. Thus, there came the power vacuum and only few people remained back to hold the political as well as economic power forming cleavage in the society.

After independence of Bangladesh rich Hindu class migrated to India leaving behind Muslim-middle class and poor muslim labourers and peasants. Under the prevailing conditions Muslim middle class came to acquire the power, Muslim Bengali political identity having its own peculiarities other parts of India, Islam came late to this region and by the time it did, it was largely through the process of filtration and infiltration that it happened. Because, Bengalis were usually converts from Hinduism, their Islam has been more liberal and tolerant of unorthodoxy than that of North-western India. A direct reinforcement took place because Islam came to Bengal through the activities of sufis. Sufism has similarity with vedanta.

Muslims of Bengal have multilinear and multidimensional divisions amongest them in particular, the ashraf / ajlaf[48] stratification, the former claiming superiority because of this extra territorial links. Among the high born

---

48. Asim Roy, "The Bengal Cultural Mediators : and the Bengal Muslim Identily, in the nineteenth and early twentieth centuries," 'South Asia,' Vol. X, No. 1, 1987. p. 214.

classes there was a tendency to discover and claim extra territiorial ancestory, which presupposes an admiration by these classes for a culture and lifestyle more akin to that of the west wing of Pakistan. The ashraf links with Afghan Islam and social superiority over other muslim Bengalis thus adds one more dimension to Bengali Islam. Such divisions later resulted in factionalism in the Bengali society.

"Bangladesh has 86.6% of muslim, population. The balance of the population is mostly Hindu (12.1%) with small Christian (0.3%), Budhist (0.6%) and animist groups. The muslims are almost all Sunnis, there are virtually no Shia, of the Ithna Ashari (Twelver Ibranin) sect and only a few followers of the Agakhan (Sevener Ismaili) sect."49

In Bangladesh secularism was introduced and was expected to succeed merely through being sanctioned by the constitution. But Islam had an ingrained and overwhelming influence on the values, norms and life-style of people in Bangladesh. In fact, most of the social forces operating within the country contribute, in some way be traced to the tenets of Islam. "A member of muslim community may be an athiest, but the social institutions, personal laws, customs, traditions, history, arts and literature which have helped to mould his individual social existence have been closely related to Islam."50

---

49. 'Bangladesh Population Censue, 1981 : Analytical Finding and National Tables' (Dhaka : Bangladesh Bureau of Statistics August, 1984). p. 75.

50. Donald Smith, "Emerging Patterns of Religion and Politics" in Donald Smith (ed.) 'South Asian Politics and Religion' (Princeton : New Jersy : Princeton University Press, 1966). p. 22

The constitution as adopted by Sheikh Mujibur Rahman, in 1972 strived to lay the foundations of a democratic-socialistic-society in Bangladesh. In the Preamble of the Constitution of People's Republic of Bangladesh adopted on 4th November 1972 it had been declared that,

"We, the people of Bangladesh, having proclaimed our independence on the 26th day of March, 1971, and through a historic struggle for national liberation, establish the independent sovereign people's Republic of Bangladesh: pledging that the high ideals of nationalism, socialism, democracy and secularism, which inspired our heroic people to dedicate themselves to, and our brave martyrs to sacrifice their lives in, the national liberation struggle, shall be the fundamental principles of the Constitution."[51]

Among the Fundamental Principles of State policy laid down in Bangladesh constitution, nationalism has been defined as:

"The unity and solidarity of the Bangla national which deriving its identity from its language and culture, attained a sovereign and independent Bangladesh through a united and determined struggle in the war of independence, shall be the basis of Bengali nationalism."[52]

The constitution of 1972 reflected popular aspiration, such as an unfettered representative democracy with guaranteed fundamental rights, independence of judiciary and socialistic society, with the state controlling the commanding heights of economy, a multifaceted rural cooperative system with a view to arising of the patterns of

---

51. Government of Bangladesh, The Constitution of the People's Republic of Bangladesh, 1972 (Dacca, 1975), pp. 1-4.

52. Ibid.

land ownership and to regulate procurement and collectisation of the produce to ensure equitable distribution, universal and compulsory primary education, non-violation of the basic tenets of Islam, no discrimination on the basis of religion or sex, an independent and non aligned foreign policy and self reliance.

Under the constitution of 1972 the military remained subbordinate to the civilian authority. President had the highest command over the armed forces. The command of army came directly into the hands of the Mujib and later in the hands of Zia as presidential system had been adopted. The military rulers did not follow the constitutional provisions in constitutional role to the military in the sphere of politics but could not succeed. The constitution was frequently changed by the military rulers to suit their interests

The leadership of the army was earlier in the hands of young officers. The leaders who participated in liberation war of Bangladesh also joined military, without much training. Such a military was a politicised military, which sought a political role in the chaotic situations. "The armed forces of Bangladesh have three main wings-Army, Airforce and Navy. Bangladesh has total active armed forces-106,500 of which, Army has 93000, Navy has 7,500 and Airforce 6000 forces. The Paramilitary forces constitute Bangladesh Rifles-30000; Armed police-5000 and Ansars 20000."[53]

After the enactment of constitution elections were held and Mujib won with the majority vote. Although the

---

53. The Military Balance, (London : 1991-92), p. 589

initital arrangements reflected a democratic polity under Mujib, but the concentration of power and authority in one-party and in one leadership later proved fatal. Mujib relied heavily on his party men, who were more interested in gaining favours and influence. The model of politics and government that Awami league regime initially followed was characterised by single dominant party system.[54] Mujib faced factionalism, corruption and violence, which became the dominant feature of his regime. It seemed that Mujibur Rahman was unable to grasp the realities of the situation and to handle the post revolutionary society. "The situation became so desparate that Mujibur Rahman who was considered by many as a great champion of democracy and free institutions trasnformed the country from a multiparty democratic system into a one party authoritarian state."[55]

The economic conditions deteriorated. Prices of grain increased rapidly, corruption violence and malpraccitices led to the collapse of law and order under such circumstances Mujib force 'Jatiyo Rakhi Bahini' which he trusted more than the army. Mujib announced the formation of Bangladesh Krishak Sramik Awani League (B.A.K.S.A.L.) Only this party was allowed to play the political role in the country. All other political parties were banned. The free press was abolished. "The transformation of Mujib the democrat, to Mujib the dictator must have been shocking to politically conscious, very intelli-

---

54. Raunaq Jahan, Bangladesh Politics : Problem and Issues. (Delhi : University Press, Ltd. 1980). p. 34.

55. Dilara Choudhry, "Challenges to Democracy in Bangladesh," Regional Studies, Vol. V, No. 1, Winter, 1986/87, p. 24.

gent and highly sensitive people of Bangladesh, who had only a short while ago made great sacrifices of liberty and equality."56

All the above factors, thus, contributed significantly for setting a stage for a group of army officers to act violently. As a result, in a military coup in August, 1975, Mujib and several of his family members were murdered by a group of young army officers.

As a leader Mujib had outstanding qualities, but he could not utilise his popularity and Chairsma in institutionalising the direct rule of military. The series of traumatic events which took place in 1975 finally brought Zia-ur-Rahman into power. Zia tried to legitimise his power, including a national referendum. He also launched his own political party B.N.P./ politician. Zia, thus, turned himself into a full fledged president under a democratic facade.

His civilianisation of regime distanced him from some of the ambitious army officers. The dilemma contributed largely to his tragic assassination in Chittagong in May 1981. After smooth succession and was elected president. But within weeks the unease of armed forces lead to Gen. Erashad's coup and to the reimposition of military rule and martial law early in 1982. Ershad during his nine year regime tried to establish individual absolutism, which abolished all the values and norms and democratic institutions. Throughout his regime the power remained in the cantonment. To secure popular support and legitimacy Ershad followed the footsteps of Zia. But his use of public office

56. S.K. Chakravarty, The Evolution of Politics in Bangladesh : 1947-1978. (New Delhi : Associated Publishing House, 1978) p. 229.

and money for his personal aggrandizement and for political patronage had gone beyond all conceivable proportions.

It is only the mass movements which have proved to be effective to do away with the autocratic regimes. As the democratic aspirations among people are hightened, the movement establishes the dictum that there is no alternative to popular mandate expressed through free and fair elections for going to power and public office and to form a popularly acceptable and legitimate government.

The book is an in-depth study on the various issues involved in the politics of Bangladesh. The efforts have been made all through to find out what remains the basis as far as the functioning of military and politics is concerned. The polity of Bangladesh has been analysed through its establishment and through the independent years for restoration and development of democratic processes at the hands of changing military and civilian regimes.

In the backdrop of the contextuality of the problem, the role of military in politics in general and in Bangladesh in particular has been studied. This will help in understanding the discrenible pattern of civil-military relations, basis of military intervention in politics and reasons for the failure of democracy. In case of Bangladesh the impact of Bangladesh nationalist movement on the role of army in its politics is important to analyse. Other issues which are important to analyse are: the impact of modernisation on the role of army in the politics of Bangladesh, the impact of modernised army on the process of socio-economic transformations, the ideology perpetuated or ascended by military rulers, the strategies applied by military rulers for legitimising their rule, the causes for unsucessaful and successful coups and counter-coups and the specific nature of Bangladesh's military establishent which led it into the sphere of politics.

For the investigation of the issues posed above, the scientific study has focused on micro as well as macro analysis of the role of military in politics. In my view it is interaction, overlapping, interlocking and interdependence of various environmental, cultural and socio-economic forces of society in relation to political sphere are important for empirical investigation. Each specific society has a structure of its own by the type of culture and socio-economic set-ups having their own type of political systems. It also gives rise to various varibles to dominate over others which determine the role of military in the sphere of politics. These facts and variables can be ascertained by empirically establishing various conditions under different situations.

The study is based on theretical as well as empirical works of eminent scholars on the subject. Though it is impossible to be free from the value biases of the researcher but a sternous effort has been made to explicit the implicit values by formulating the scientific schemes of chapterisation.

The first Chapter 'Introduction' provides in overview of the topic, right from its inception various factors innolveed in the politics of Bangladesh, which shape up the polity of country around civil-military lelations and the importance of democracy have been discussed.

The next chapter, 'Theoretical Questions' deals with the review of existing theories on the role of military in politics in general and in Bangladesh in particular. The hypothesis and inferences have also been drawn after critical evaluation of the available literature. This is necessary for our investigation of the problem. Construction of theory is important for explaining and defining the concept. The working definition can be obtained and a definite course can be chartered out only after proving the theoretical questions. Theoretical questions will help cummulatively in micro as well as macro analysis.

The third chapter 'Historical Background' analyses the ideological and cultural foundation of the nationalist movement and the role of armed bands in nationalist liberation movement which assumed language question from 1948-54, federal balance and regional autonomy from 1954-65 and national liberation movement from 1965-71. This chapter also deals with formation of social forces such as military, armed bands and political resistence movements which emerged in the liberation struggle of Bangladesh. The chapter also tries to get to the roots of the relations between civilian society and armed bands and also military and armed bands in historical perspective. Histoicity of the problem is important for fourmulating analytical freamework for the understanding of political phenomenon. Because men, groups, nations do not act only as they want to, but are also conditioned by historical circumstances.

"Army and Political Institutions" explains the nature and characteristics of political institutions i.e., executives, legislatives, jidiciary, parliament, political parties, pressure groups bureaucracy etc., and their relations with army. The chapter also takes into account the level of political culture.

The army rule does not operate in vacuum, it is a product of definite socio-economic set up. Therefore, the next chapter, 'Army and socio-economic modernisation' deals with the level of socio-economic development of Bangladesh society and the level of modernisation of Bangladesh army. It also analyses the role of army as an instrument of socio-economic modernisation and impact of modernisation on the nature of military organisation.

The last chapter, 'Military establishment' tries to explore the military establishment variables such as ideology, recruitment, training, social composition and representativeness, level of factionalism, level of professionalisation, level of factionalism, level of techincal know-how etc., as the basis for fascilitating or retarding the role of military in the politics of Bangladesh. The chapter explains the very nature of military establishment in Bangladesh. It evaluates the role of civil-military relations, including the causes for coups and counter coups, the military's espousing cause for promoting the popular rule and the natures of conflict. While external factors like political institutions and socio-economic changes act merely as catalytic agents, the bases of involment of military into the political spheres lie within itself.

All the chapters cover the media's role in various areas and in various form amidst the ongoing process of socio-economic and political chenges, which are disectly selated to the role of military in general and to the case of Bangladesh in particular.

The conclusions and the finding have been summarised at the end by drawing a picture of generalisations explaining the nature and direction to the politics and military in Bangladesh.

The secondary sources include the published material, such as books, articles, research journals, autobiographies, magazines and published material in news papers, which are concerned with to the role of military in general and in particular in Bangladesh. The military's espousing cause for promoting the popular rule and the natures of conflict. While external factors like political institutions and socio-economic changes act merely as catalytic agents, the bases of involment of military into the political spheres have direct effect on media and its role.

II-Theoretical Questions

Theoretical Prespective provides a significant guideline for objective conduct of research by pointing the areas that are likely to be fruitful, that is, areas in which meaningful relationships among variables are likely to be found. If insignificat variables are located, the research will be sterile no matter how meticulous the observations and inferences be.

A theoretical perspective gives meaning to the facts to be studied. It provides the researcher with a definit view point i.e., a direction which in the long way helps us to enquire into relationaship between certain variables selected from infinite array of variables. The theoretical survey helps to organise the various facts related to our investigation. Moreover, theory summarizes known facts and even predicts facts which have not yet been observed or explored. In other words, it helps in pointing out the gaps in our knowledge. Needless to say that such gaps would not be visible if our facts are not systematised and organised.

The scientific study needs to enquire not only the analysis on mcro as well as macro level, but also their inter-relationship. For objective study, the implicit subjective orientation has to be made explicit. Thus, the explainatory framework is necessary for analytical purpose as well as for solving the problem.

After the second world war most of the colonised nations got freedom. These nations were marked by horizontal and vertical cleavages in their socio-political and socioeconomic planes. The linguistic, religious, ethnic and regional cleavages gave rise to fissiparous tendencies which threatened the national unity of all these new states. Also, the new nations had weak democratic traditions and a limited experience of running democratic institutions. And, the indigenous political culture had been authoritarian in its contents, right from the institutions of faimly.

The leaders of these newly independent states followed the westernised modernisation steps in order to ensure political stablity and development. But this path proved to be hazardous, as the traditional ethos came into conflict with the forces of unistitional ethos came into conflict with the forces of unistitutionalised modernization and created stresses and strains in the existing political and social structure. The new nations lacked both much wanted well organised political parties and competent political leadership.

In this backdrop, within the decade or so of the establishment of these new nations as sovereign states, most of them collapsed and settled under authoritarian military regimes. And, with the same frequency with which most of countries had attained independence, went under the military rule, causing a death blow to the democratic institutions. At this juncture serious efforts were made by various scholars regarding the role of military in politics. A broad survey of the vast literature available on the role of military in the politics of developing countries can be grouped under two schools braodly (though there are large variations), one, which explains the phenomenon in the nature of military establishment itself while the other school explains it in the context of socio-economic developments, aspects of political development and foreign influence, i.e., the causes lie out side the internal nature of military establishment. Both these schools are neither exclusive nor inclusive. They overlap each other in explaining the phenomenon. A third sub-school of the latter interprets this phenomenon in terms of class cleavages in the society.

Some of the important works of first school may be attributed to Harold Lasswell[1], Morris Janowitz[2], Bengt Abrahamsson[3], William R. Thompson[4], Lucian Pye[5] and G. Mirsky.[6] All these emphasised on the sensitivity of military elite to the socio-economic and political changes in the society.

---

1. Harold lasswell, The Garrison state hypothesis To-day 'in Huntington's (ed) The Changing Patterns of Military Politics (Glencoe : Free Press, 1962)

2. Morris Janowitz, The Military in the Political Development of New Nations (Chicago : The University of Chicago Press, 1964.) and The Professional Soldier : A Social and Political Portrait (New York : The Free Press, 1960.)

3. Bengt Abrahamsson, Military Professionalisation and Political Power, (London : Sage Publications, 1962.)

4. William R. Thompson, The Grievances of Coup-markers, (London : Sage Publications, 1973.)

5. Lucian Pye in J.J. Johnsons (ed) "The Role of Military in Underdeveloped Countries" (New Jersey : Princeton University Press, 1964.)

6. G. Mirsky, "The Political Role of the Army in Asian and African countries" in Social Science Today. No. 2, 1969.

The Peculiar aspects of military organisation reveal about tht role of military in politics. For example, what purposes d o o fficers se e a s a ppropriate t o t he a rmed forces? If they view their mission as protecting the nation from external invasions, They also see that the nation should be protected internally against the corrupt politicians. Put in different words, the ideological orientation of military elite accelarate or retard the stepping in process of military in civilian arena. The nature and extent of political awareness amongst armed forces also draws them towards active involvement in politics. Sometimes, the cleavages, which exist within the armed forces, whether founded in class or ethnic origins, in the differences inherent in specialised branches of military, in types of professional training or in some other factor, they may become so divisive that they result in intervention. Thus, ideology, recruitment, organisation, socio-economic stauts of military, have to be taken into consideration while evaluating the role of military in politics.

The propunders of second school are : Samuel P. Huntington[7], S.E. Finer[8], Edward Shils[9], Henry Bienen[10],

---

7. For detail see; Samuel P. Huntington, Political Order in Changing Societies (New Haven : Yale Universtity Press, 1968.)

8. S.E. Finer, The man on the Horseback : The Role of Military in Politics (Harmondsworth : Penguin Books, 1975.)

9. Edward Shils, "The Military in the Political Development of the new states in John J. Johnson (ed.) Role of Military in Underdeveloped Countries (New Jersey : Princeton Press, 1962.)"

10. Henry Bienen (ed.) The Military Intervenes : Case Studies in Political Development (New York : Russell Sage Fundation, 1968) and The Military and the Modernisation (Chicago & New York : Aldine Atherton, 1971)

Horwitz[11] etc... The various factors grouped under the second set of variables namely, external or environmental variables involve- political democratic traditions, level of political institutionlalisation, level of political culture, role of military in the mintenance of law and order, the performance and legitimacy of the government, the actions of civilian leaders, politicisation of various sections of classes of society, the extent of soci-economic modernisation and economic growth.

Harold lasswell[12] was the propounder of first school. He emphasised on "Garrison State." The rise of "Garrison State" was a counter produce of the rise of totalitarianism in eastern Europe. It was also the by product of technological innovation in arms and amunition. Lasswell attributed increasing role of military in politics to the domination of violence in world politics, Since, military monopolises the instrument of violence, the role of military in politics became inevitable. In Lasswell's 'Garrison State' authority was "dictatorial, governmentalised, centralized and integrated."[13] In brief, Lasswell regarded military of the organised means of violence and warfare. The military used the massive socio-politcal and economic resources to enhance their status. It, therefore, came to occupy the pivotal role in the society.

Lasswell's findings do not reveal the sequential facts as seventeenth and eighteenth century was dominated more

---

11. Irving L. Horowitz, Three Worlds of Development (New York : Oxford University Press, 1966.)

12. Harold Lasswell, op.cit. pp. 55-70

13. Reymond Aron, 'Remarks on Lasswell's Garrison Stage Armed Forces and Society, Vol. V, No. 3, Spring, 1979, p. 347.

by military elites than civilians. For Lasswell, military rule was a totalitarian rule. His prediction of emergence of totalitarianism or centralisation in world politics seems to be fallacious as most of the countries in nineties are adhering more to democratic norms. Lasswell inhereted biases in his analysis by attributing increasing military role in politics as manifestation of rise of the totalitarian politics in the world. But he failed to explain the democratic thrust of western democracies. No doubt, the contribution of Lasswell lies in his finding of monopoly over the instruments of violence which could be an only variable for military intervention.

Janowitz[14] is more objective in his analysis, since his analysis are neither closed nor open. He used various nuances in evaluating the role of military in politics. organisation and responsiveness of military to technological and political changes, Janwitz suggests a new framework for the operation of the military in modern times. He formulated five models to cover the civil-military relations.[15] Out of the five, first three exist prior to the establishement of military rule. These are (i) Authoritarian Personal control (ii) Authoritarian mass party and (iii) Democratic competetive. In all these three cases military's role in politics is limited. In the other two models military played a greater role political affairs. They are (iv) Civil-military coalition and (v) Military oligarchy. Janowitz exphasises that after the military takeovers, military tries to build a broader political apparatus by includ

14. Janowitz, The Military in the Politics of New nations : An Essay in Comparative Analysis, Op. cit.

15. Ibid. pp. 5-18.

ing either its own personnel or even civilians, but the whole apparatus remains dominated by military.

Janowitz relates the role of armed forces to the level of political culture. The role of military also depends on the nature of national liberation movements and the involvement of military in these movements. The role of military in the politics of Bangladesh can be analysed in this perspective.

While analysing the comparative military behaviour of new nations Janowitz focuses on their common goals of modernisation and social change. He feels that there are a variety of common organisational features in the militarys of new nations which condition or limit the capacity of the military profession to exercise political power.

Janowitz is of the view, that the capacity of military establishment to intervene in the domestic politics of new nations is derived from its distinct organistional format : its control of the instruments of violence, its ethos of public services, national integration and its skill structure. which combines managerial skills with heroic posture. Its unified organisation contributes to strong internal cohesion, which is reinforced by successful operational experience, whether in the case of ex-colonial armies that fought in world-war II or post liberation armies that gathered experience in internal constabulary operations against dissident groups.[16]

In most of the developing countries the army organises elite troops, which are deployed at strategic

---

16. Ibid. pp. 32-34.

points of the capital city for the purposes of security against internal disturbances. Thus, the political role of military is closely linked to the orgainsation of police having internal as well as external forces. The frequent use of military in internal politics in new nations is, thus, one of the causes of military intervention in politics.

The skill structure[17] and career lines of the military also develop political orientation among them. The unique and specialised career opportunities of modern armies develop small groups of officers, more politically oriented to give rise to military bureaucracy, which has its own leaders, who link military bureaucracy whith political elites.

The nature of recruitment[18] in military also has a powerful influence on the political behaviour of armies. The military in new nations was largely recruited from middle and lower middle class groups who could fit easily into the divide and rule tactics of colonial masters. Some aristocratic elements were also recruited, as in the case of the families of north-west frontier and Punjab in the (British) Indian army, to the exclusion of nationalist elements, such as the politically conscious Bengalis.

After the end of colonial rules, in the new nations military bacame the symbol of sovereignty because of their education, training, experience and skill, which mobilised it for achieving rapid social change in their nations by coming directly into the politics of these nations.

Janowitz does not employ a static ideal type analysis of civil-military relations rather, he proposes a politically sensitive profession integrated with the society. He treats

---

17. Ibid. pp. 40-45.
18. Ibid, pp. 50-60.

military as a social system in which, he takes professional characteristics as variables interacting with eash other and with external conditions.[19]

As Arthur D. Larson[20] points that Janowitz model fails to clearly delineate the boundaries of military progessionalism, he also does not discuss how that professionalism is to retain its uniqueness under the pressure towards civilisation or its members, their expertise and detachment, with the heavy emphases on political sensitivity and indoctrinaion which he proposes.

In the similar vein, Edwin Lieuwen took organisational point from Janowitz and possession of arms from Lasswell, but Lieuwen emphasizes purely on comparative administrative organisational structure of military than on sociology of the organisation. He puts the matter bluntly, "In terms of political institutions, there is no political civilian force or combination of forces able to compete with the armed forces, once that institution makes up its mind on a given issue nothing can prevent it from having its way.. This is largely because military has arms, a monopoly on the means of violence and thus the incontrovertible argument of forces on its side. But it is also because the military possesses an organisational structure superior to that of any civilian political party. Its centralised command,

---

19. Quoted in Veena Kukreja, Civil Military Relations in Developing Countries, India Quartierly, Vol. XLV, No. 2 & 3, April-Sep, 1989, p- 167.

20. Arthur D. Larson as Quoted by Veena Kukreja in Ibid.

21. For detail see : Edwin Lieuwen, General v/s. Presidents :

New-militarism in Latin America. (New York : Fredrick A Praeger, 1964) its hierarchical structure, and its disciplined membership makes it capable of acting with complete unity."22

Jacques Van Doorn[23] belives that military profession plays an important role in military interventions. If a civilian society is to retain dominance over military, it can not afford to neglect the effects of professionalisation as they are more deeply involved in the political process. Professionalisation creates experts, who have direct implications for the social power. Van Doorn has stated, "the concept of military professionalism, like every other king of professionalism, includes a perennial search for autonomy, which is, in contradition to tight political control."[24] Doorn's views are contradictory to the views of S.P. Huntington. In the case of Huntingion, progessionalism leads to non- involvement in civilian affairs whereas, according to Doorn military's involvement in civilian affairs is a by-product of its professionalism.[25]

Pye[26] in the fashion of Lasswell but in different context analyses the military's role as product of demonatrative effect of world politics, which resulted in cumulative effect in internal politics. Pye considers military political development in new nations because only military organisations are secular, differentiated and integrated.

---

22. Ibid. P. 97.

23. For Details see : Jacques Van Doorn, Political Change and the Control of the Military in Janowitz (ed.) Military Profession and Military Regimes (Mouton : Hague, 1969.)

24. Ibid, p. 12

25. For Huntington's views see page.

26. Lucian Pye, Op. cit.

Armies of the new nations have been influenced by western military technology. They are equipped with modern training and skill. Thus, military elites become more ambitious than civilians for seeing their societies as modern societies. Thus, modern training and skill have its implications for assuming political roles.

Military's more exposure to the outside world, make the army leaders of new nations sensitively aware of the extent to which their countries are economically and techonologically underdeveloped. Thus military has greater awareness of international standards and greater sensitivity to weaknesses in their own society even when they stand at some distance from their civilian society even when they stand at some distance from their civilian socieitise. Armies in newly emergent countries provide a sense of citizenship and an appreciation of political action. In some cases it can lead to a more responaible nationalism and to the process of nation-building.

Pye has broadly identified three categories of civilnilitary relations.[27] In the first category military remains out because only political order and not social order is disrupted. In the second category military monopolises the political arena while espusing for the development of democracy. In the third category democratic functioning stops and army assumes all administrative roles. According to Pye, only military organisations can functions as modernising agents in new nation-states because a modern nation state needs a class of competent administrators who work as responsible and skilled politicans for national development. Pye attributed mili-

---

27. Ibid. pp. 84-85.

tary intervention to the demonstrative effect of the Western countries where as Lasswell attributed to Eastern European countries. But both these scholars failed to understand that demonstrative effects always do not lead to penetrative effect. Sometimes, it may lead to reactive effect too.

The n ation o f m ilitary p rofessionalism o f B engt Abrahamsson[28] has great functional adaptability. Putting in defferent words the modernisation capacited military to expertize are major factors underlying both the military's normative influence and its political power, Military's normative influence establishes the military as an important pressure group leading to high technological development and enables the military to become proficient in the utilisation of public relations and propaganda. Military's involvement in rapid expansion of modernisation of weapons and equipment provides it a direct power potential.

Abrahamsson gives three reasons for military's extended political roles.[29] First, the growing complexity of modern warfare. Second, deployment of army in many new areas for defence purposes during wars. Third, specially in the post world war-II period, military has assumed a number of ancillary function's as for e.g. administration of occupied countries, police tasks, counter guerilla warfare and training of foreign troops in civil action.

Professionalism in military, says Abrahamsson, leads to the creation of corporate cohesion and solidarity which leads it to political power resulting in collision with civil

---

28. Bengt Abrahamsson, op. cit.
29. Ibid. p. 155.

ian authority. He rejects Huntington's argument both logically and empirically which says that professionalism induces the military towards a low political posture. Abrahamsson does not agree with Huntington on the contention that professionalism involves political sterility.

Like Janowitz and Abrahamsson, G. Mirsky[30] emphasises on military organisation, which facilitates military to play an active role in politics, but highlights the rise of military bureaucracy and its implication on the role of military. Like any other bureauracy, military bureaucracy too have tendency to isolate and to dominate rest of the population. The features of "praetorianism" are secondary variables which induce army to come into politics. Mirsky exphasised on the disciplined and centralised leadership provided by military. The military institutions and organisations play a dominant role in shaping the destiny of a nation by promoting a road of socio-economic development.

Common features of army which result in political action are-a hierarchy of ranks, military discipline, an oath of allegiance, regulations etc. Military comes to play its role only in the societies in which the political system is about to collapse or has collapsed. Societal factors are, thus, the conditions for germinating military coups.

The reasons for the coups[31] which Mirsky has grouped are (i) the presence of a nationalistic dissatisfaction in a society (ii) a long drawn out inner political crisis (iii) dissatisfaction of educated elite and (iv) inefficiency

---

30. G. Mirsky, Op. cit.

31. Ibid, pp. 83, 84.

of the civilian government, combined with corrupt administration.

Mirsky agrees with janowitz for making a mass political apparatus beyong their own organisational structure after the military has taken to political power. Mirsky, however, feels that military in politics can play an effectives role only it it adopta a socialist ideology.

William R. Thompson[32] has made an attempt to explain the occurances of military coups and counter-coups. He attributed military's role in politics to the lack of basic ementies and flaws in military organisation. He has distinguished mainly two types of grievances[33] (i) Corporate and (ii) Not-so-corporate.

The needs of military ogranisation include-autonomy, heirarchical discipline, functional monopoly, security, prestige, honour and an adequate level of supply of inputs, such as men, equipment training and finacial support. Morecover military perceives its polition vis-a-vis other organisations within the country and foreign competitive country. And, when its demands are not fulfilled, they add to the corporate grievances of military which result in coup.

In the not-so-corporate grivances, there are greater chances of military coups. The personnel engaged in coup activity have personal, functional and sectional causes are implicit in coups but, not-so-corporate reasons are made explict in coups. Military personnel have their own conceptions of what is proper for their organisational welfare and regime-military relations, when a serious antago

---

32. William R. Thompson, Op. cit.

33. Ibid. pp. 12.31.

nism is developed in their own and civilian conceptions, the chances of military interventions increase. Thomson's analysis is partial as it fails to explain the intricate dynamics of civil-military relations. Military intervention is not confined only to corporate or not-so-corporate causes.

The following writers explain the problem of role of military in politics in the context of the environmental condition rather than on the nature of military itself. Thus, they take nature of military as a by-prouduct of environmental factors. These writers do not exclude the nature of military establishment variables as factors for military intervention but give primacy to environmental set-up.

Edward Shils[34] while accounting for the prominence of the military in Asian and African societies says that, the ascendency of military in the domestic life of these states has been a response to the difficultic life of these states has been a response to the difficulties which the new nation have encountered in their efforts to establish themselves as modern sovereignities. The new nations are plagued by various weaknesses, which are not compensated by the political institutions, inhereted or established at the time of independence. These political institutions were mainly parliamentary, more or less democratic and liberal. Military rule became one of several practicable and apparently stable alternatives to these unstable institutions.

The elities of these developing nations put forward the modernisation as their main objective. The modernising process dislocated the traditional power structure and no other alternate modern struture could fill

34. Edward Shils, op. cit. pp. 7-67.

up the gap in these societies. Thus, under the situtions of anarchy, chaos, instablity, corruption and under developmentm military stepped into the politics of these new nations as a modernising force. Shils analysis do not explain the non-military democratic regimes of underdeveloped countries, which have almost similar environmental conditions but are modernising themselves according to democratic norms without military's interferences.

The other profound spokesman of the environmental school is Samuel. P. Huntington.[35] According to him the causes which lead military to play role in politics basically lie not in the nature of military organisation itself rather, it is the specific manifestation of a broader phenomenon in the politics of underdeveloped nations, which he called, "praetorianism" "Praetoianwhich" refers to the general politicisation of social forces and institutions. In such a society, all sorts of political institutions and groups become directly engaged in the general politics in the marked absence of autonomy, complexity, coherence and adaptability of political institutions. In such societies, not only armies but also clergies, labour unions, universities, bureaucracies and other groups get politicised.

Huntington correlates the role of military in politics to the level of political development. He defines political development in terms of political institutiona-lisation vis-a-vis mass mobilisation and political participation. The military institutions in developing countries are more adaptive, cohesive, complex and coherent as compared to the civil institutions. Thus, military institutions become potential contenders for power.

---

35. S.P.Huntington, Political Order in Changing Societis. Op. cit.

Huntington puts that rise of military professionalism is inversely related to military intervention. Because, the development of professional ethic leads military towards the task ensuring national security. The more is the military professionalised, the more it is subservient to civilian authority. Huntington discusses two types of civilian control[36]: Subjective and objective. Subjective control involves maximisation of the power of one or more civilian groups over the military, thereby reducing its autonomy. The civilian control in the objective sense is the maximisation of military professionalism i.e. militarisation of the military. In short, subjective control implies the effort of civilian groups to restrict military autonomy, while objective control is aimed at widening it. In the first case civilian control is ensured by the political pressure from civilian groups in the second, the control is guaranteed by the military itself, provided it is properly professionalised.

The military Juntas, coups and dictatorships result because the slow process of political institution building results in the necessity for social reform and the military officers under such conditions view themselves as modernisers per excellence, But at the same time, they are indifferent or hostile to the needs of political institution building and they are ill prepared to make fundamental changes in political process. Military Juntas or coups may, thus, spur modernisation but they can not produce a stable political order. Thus, Huntington does not consider military institution as an agent of development, but conditions it with the rate of social mobilisation and political

36. Huntington in The Soldier and the State. Op. cit. pp. 80-83.

participation. Huntington is self contradictory because he attributes military intervention to comparative superiority of its institutions to civil institutions in terms of adaptability, complexity and autonomy yet he doubts its stability.

On the whole, Huntington's contribution to the theory of civil-military relations related to political institutionalisation remains highly valuable. Four aspects[37] of civil-military relations, which he posted are highly valuable. First, that military officers and civilians constitute disctinct groups. Second, the relation between these groups are inherently conflictual in nature. Third, he held that keeps the conflict within bounds is subordination of officers corps to civilian except on matters requiring military expertise. Finally, he perceived shifts in civil-military relations over time as a function of the degree of effectiveness of civilian control.

These fundamental notions of civil-military relations given by Huntington have not been challenged even by the theorists who have subsequently found fault with his analysis. Janowitz objects on his 'objective' institutional constraints as a determinent of civilian control, but otherwise accepted the general conceptual framework advanced by Hungtington. Bengt Abrahamsson[38] questioned Huntington's linkage of military professionalisation and political neutrality, but agreed with the general framework given by Huntington. Writers such as, Eric A.

---

37. Ibid, pp. 80-81.
38. Bengt Abrahamsson, Op. cit. p. 169.

Nordlinger[39], Amos Parlmutter[40] and Calude E. Weich Jr. and Arthor K. Smith[41] implicity adopted the position that Huntington's conceptual ideas do not offer much insight into the behaviour of military, Yet they relied heavily on his concepts to define the basic character of 'praetorianism', Eric. A nordlinger[42], for instance has described praetorianism as the antithesis of civilian control and has argued that it arises when there is conflict between soldiers and civilian government that leads to breakdown of civilian supremacy. Nordlinger points out, that coups entail immediate and fundamental changes in regime structure, the praetorians based on three different roles assumed by the military when it intervenes. He calls them as moderates, guardians and rulers in order of increasing role of military in political sphere.

Roy Macridis and steven Burg[44] lay down the conditions under which militaries may come to play political role. First, when there is a beak down process of community life. Secondly, when there is conflict over the distribution of goods to army. Thirdly, military may intervene to protect the existing social and economic 'status-quo',

---

39. Eric. A. Nordlinger, Soldier in Politics : Military Coups and Governments (New Jersy : Englewood Cliff, Prentice Hall, 1977.)

40. Amos Perlumtter, The Military and Politiccs in Modern Times. (New Haven : Yale University Press, 1977.)

41. Claude E. Welch and Arthor K. Smith (eds) Military Role and Rule (North Soititule mess : Duxbury Press, 1974.)

42. Eric. A. Nordlinger, Op. cit. p. 121.

43. Ibid. pp. 144-148.

44. Roy Macridis and Steven Burg, Introduction to Comparative Politics (New York : Harper Collins, 1991), pp. 133-134.

Finally, military heroics may tempt them to intervene and establish a military rule.

Macridis and Bury point out that the armies that intervene in politics in the contemporary era and the states in which army intervention occurs are called "praetorian" armies and praetorian states and thus they say that in praetorian states army not only has the potential to dominate the system but also has the disposition to dominate.

Amos perlmutter[45] agrees with Huntington, Nordlinger and Macridis & Bury that praetorianism induces military to intervene in politics. Most of the authoritarian and autocratic military regimes are found in societies undergoing change and lacking legitimate political order and support.

Military regimes, says Perlumtter, are n ot p urely military in composition. Instead, there is fusion between military and civilians. In such regimes, governmental authority resides in a coalition of the military and civilians, bureaucrats, managers, politicians and technocrats.

He distinguishes five types[46] of military regimes depending upon civil-military relations (i) the corpora

---

45. For Detail See : Amos Perlumtter & Valerie Plane Bonnett (ed.) The Political Influence of the Military (London : Yale Univeristy Press, 1980). Also See; Amos Perlumutter, "Civil-Military Relations in Socialist Authoritarian and Praetorian States : Prospects and Retrospects" in Roman Kolkowicz and Andrez (ed.) Soldiers. Peasents and Bureaucrats, (Boston : George Allen and Unwin, 1982) and Amos Perlumtter, "The Comparative Analysis of Military Regimes," World Politics, Vol. XXXIII, No. 1, Oct. 1980, pp. 97-120.

46. For Detail see; Amos Perlmutter, "The Comparative Analysis of Military Regimes, Op. cit p 101."

tive military regime (ii) the market bureaucratic military regime (iii) the socialistic and oligarchical military regime (iv) the army-party military regime and (v) the tyrannical military regime. Perlmutter contends that the different types of regimes in praetorian societies are the result of various kinds of coalitions.

Claude E. Welch[47] and Arthur K. Smith in the similar vein reveal that praetorianism leads to the increasing role of military in politics are (i) the extent and nature of political participation of the populace (ii) the strength of civil institutions (iii) military strength (iv) the nature of military's institutional boundaries. The military intervention of politics arises primarily from the limited or declining legitimacy of civilian political institutions. According to Claude and Smith the military regimes are found in new nations for ensuring political stablity and nation-building. The military rule become a necessity for national development, so the power by military elites should not be viewed as particularly illegitimate. Claude has also put an emphasis on organisation of military and on military's training and expertise which facilitate military to come into politics. By assigning a positive or legitimate role to military in politics Claude and Smith some what negate the urge of man for freedom or 'self-rule.'

S.E. Finer[49] agrees to the fact that armed forces enjoy three massive political advantages over civilian organisations-a marked superiority in organisation, a

---

47. Claude E. Welch and Arthur K. Smith, Op. cit.

48. Ibid. p. 89.

49. Samuel E. Finer, The Man on the Horseback : The Role of the Military in politics Op. cit.

highly emotionalised symbolic status and a monopoly of arms.[50] But he says, the moral authority for its actions is sought by the military from its society. And how far people recognise it depends upon the level of public attachment to civilian institutions, i.e. the political culture.

He distinguished four types[51] of political culture on the level of public attachment to civilian institutions. The countries having very high mobilisation are actually immune from military take overs. In such societies intervention by military is regarded as an unwarrantable intrusion e.g. Britain, U.S.A., Canada, Switzerland, Australia and New Zealand. These countries are termed as having mature political culture.

In some countries like Germany, France, U.S.S.R. and Japan military would have to reckon with strong public resistence to military interventions. Such societies are termed as having developed political culture. The countries with relatively narrow and weakly organised public and institutions will not be very resistive to military interventions, such societies have low political culture for e.g. Turkey, Argentina, Spain, Eqypt, Syria, Pakistan, Bangladesh etc. There are also the countries like Haiti and Congo in which any government can ignore the public opinion because these countries have weak political organisation. These are countries with minimal political culture.

Finer links the propensity for military's role in politics with social and economic under-development. He argues that, the propensity for military intervention is likely

---

50. Ibid. pp. 5-10.
51. Ibid, pp 78-80.

to decrease with increased social mobilisation. This view of finer is contradictory to Huntington's view that increased social mobilisation results in military interventions. Finer's concept of social mobilisation refers to such development of mony economy and increased participation in social and political activities and associations. Finer, however, lays emphasis on the fact that 'where public attachment to civilian institutions is strong, military intervention in politics will be weak and where public attachment to civilian institutions is weak or non-existent, military intervention in politics will find wide scope both in manner and in substance. Finer puts more emphasis on political culture of the societies rather than on the building of political institutions. Hower his classic work remains an organic part of general theory of civilmilitary relations.

Henry Bienen[52] believes that military plays role in politics in order to modernise the societies of new nations. Like Perlmutter, Bienen also believes that military takes part in politics through alliances and coalitions. Marion. J. Levy[53], also says that armed force organisations for modernising and ordering the society. Being m odernised o rganisation a s c ompared to other oraganisations armed forces are a ladder of social mobility.

---

52. Henry Bienen (ed.) The Military Intervenes : Case Studies in Political Development. Op. cit.

53. Marion J. Levy, Modernisation and the Structure of the Societies (Princeton N. J. : Princeton University Press, 1966)

Martin C. Needler[54] in his analysis while considering military as a modernising force combines organisational and environmental factors. But he does not consider military as a homogenous organisation as coups result due to factionalism in the organisations.

Guy Pauker[55] makes an argument about the role of military in the South-East Asian countries, as these countries experienced political instability because their leaders had neither the prestige of traditional aristocrats nor the prestige of the first generation nationalist leaders. In the absence of well established and efficient democratic government and administration, armed corps could easily come into the political sphere.

A frequent explanation of military interventions and coups in new nations is that the military constitutes a functional alternative to civil administration. Horowitz states that, "the rapidity of the developmental process guarntees the absence of well organised, popularly controlled political parties. In the absence of such parties and at times of crisis, the armed forces may be the only group capable of maintaining political order or preparing the ground for further economic break throughs. Thus, the military tends to perform all sorts of omnibus functions, paramount of which is direct political role."[56]

---

54. Martin C. Needler, "Political Development and Military Intervention in Latin America" in Henry Bienen (ed) The Military and Modernisation (New York & Chicago : Aldine Atherton Inc. 1971.)

55. Guy Pauker, South-East Asia as a Problem area in the next Decade" World Politics. Vol. Xi, April, 1959, pp. 339-345.

56. Irving L Horowitz, Three Worlds of Development op. cit. p. 59.

So far as social setting is concerned, it needs to be further atressed that democracy can not sustain in a society where large middle class is absent. Robert Putman agrees with Moshe Lissak who claims, "If a middle class is absent or its growth and quest for self experession are severely carved, the stage would be set for the emergence of the military as an alternative political power." Putman also substantiated the views of Germane and Silvert that, "military intervention is inhibited by the rise of middle strata in the social structure, since this middle strata have in special measure both the motivation and the ability to create and sustain stable civilian political institutions."[58] These authors also argue that the likelihood of military intervention is greater, the greater the cleavages and less the consensus in a society.

Most of the literature which we have evaluated deals with the general theoretical proposition of phenomena but there are very few scholars who have analysed the role of military in the politics of Bangladesh. Though generalisation is important for further investigation, pecularity of the country's polity can not be ignored for objective study. In the following pages an attempt has been made to link the macro-analysis with the micro-analysis of the polity of Bangladesh.

---

57. Robert Putman, "Towards Explaining Military Intervention in Latin America", World Politics, Vol. XX, No. 1, April, 1967 p. 957.

58. Ibid.

Veena Kukreja[59] has emphasised on civil-military relations in general as well as in Bangladesh in particular. She has given three models of civil-military relations in general; (i) Western model : this model refers to the industrial societies of Western Europe, in which military is neither expected nor is it oriented to intervene. (ii) establishing the supremacy of civilian party over the military. (iii) Praetorian Model : Under this the armed forces are more likely to come into politics. Military mainly comes into politics by forming alliances with other civilian groups such as bureaucracies, elites etc.

The variables of civil-military relations as discussed are (i) the level of institutionalisation of civilian political procedures such as level of political institutionalisation, legitimacy, level of mass political mobilisation and participation, role of political leadership and political parties and functioning of democratic institutions. (ii) The level of military institutionalisation it takes into account the size, defence expenditure, recruitment, cohesiveness, autonomy, professionalisation and resources as factors that affect the realtion strength or weakness of military institutions vis-a-vis civilian institutions. (iii) The third variable stands for domestic socio-economic environment and

---

59. Veena Kukreja, "Civil Military Relations - in developing Countries," India Quarterly Vol. XLV, No. 2 & 3, April Sep, 1989 and also see, Veena Kukreja, Civil Military Relations in South Asia: Pakistan. Bangladesh & India (New Delhi : Sage Publications, 1991.)

60. Hamza Alvi, "The State in post-colonial Societies : Pakistan and Bangladesh" in K. Gough and H.P. Sharma (eds) "Imperialism and Revolution in South Asia" (New York : Monthly Review Press, 1973.)

within the military and civilian institutions which interact with each other and struggle for dominance. (iv) The nature of boundaries refers to clarity of demarcation of civil and military institutions.

The study of civil-military relations in the particular case of Bangladesh has been made by taking the four summary variables. Military in Bangladesh came to play its role due to low level of democratic political institutions, less organised political parties, weak economy and high level of social mobilisation. The military was highly politicised as most of military men were freedom fighters. Many a times military was called to aid the civil authorities in situations of political crisis and natural disasters. Military adopted various strategies and tactics once they seized power. The strategies and tactics have been listed as-elimination of opposition political parties, faith in Islam, formation of patrimonial political parties, holding of referendums etc. Veena kukreja's work provides a good insight of the civil-military relations in general and in the particular case of Bangladesh are missing which could further help in understanding military interventions by explaining the releationships between the rulers and the ruled.

Hamza Alvi tries to explain military phenomenon in the context of class struggle. Alvi points out that the role of the bureaucrat-military oligarchy in post-colonial societies is datermined within the matrix of a class society. He distinguishes three propertied classes[61] in a society the metropolitan bourgeoisie, the indigenous bourgeoisie and landed class. Political and social tensions in

61. Ibid. P. 148.

Bangladesh were mainly because of the twin factors of disparity.discontent. The ruling circle os businessmen or bureaucrats (civil and military) landowners and politicians, favour actions which aggravate the disparities and result in military and bureaucracy's enhanced role in politics. But Alvi failed to analyse the antagonism among various upper class segments which may be inhibitious for military intervention.

The Four main reasons for the failure of democracy and for the rise of military rule in Bangladesh as listed by Dilara Choudhury[62] were : lack of democractic tradition, lack of well organised political parties, the role of civilinception was not imbibed with democratic values and principles. The colonial democracy failed to develop a genuine egalitarian spirit which could be regarded as the foundation of liberal political ethos. The political parties were not fully organised and lacked democratic orientation and experience. They clustered around leadership rather than on any programme or ideology. Political parties got engaged in sectarian interests and corruption. Bangladesh like many other third world countries inherited the civil-military infrastructure based on the experience of colonialism in which military occupied a very prestigious place and contributed to safeguard the nation in deterioration of economic and political conditions. The Bangladesh army was a politicised army. After the assassination of Mujib, the political vacuum offered a clear path for the military to intervene in politics.

---

62. Dilara Choudhury, "Challenges to democracy in Bangladesh," Regional Studies. Vol. V, No. 1, Winter, 1986/87, pp. 23-33.

Like Dilara, M. Nazrul Islam[63] attributed the role of military in politics to lack of effective party system in Bangladesh. The other factors which he gave included dictatorial tendencies of Mujib which he gave included dictatorial tendencies of Mujib which alienated the military bureaucracy, reduction of defence expenditure by Mujib. The discontentment which resulted from the process of alienation finally paved way to a military regime supported by civil-bureaucracy. Nazrul Islam says that military has been able to work in the politics of Bangladesh as there exists a gross lack of consensus on state ideology, the form of government and the type of economy the country should have. Ceaseless debate and doubts over the role of the dominant institutional groups, intense factionalism in party politics and inadequate growth of institutions, exclusiveness of ruling elites and the question over their legitimacy have perpetuated a situation of serious political unrest and instablity.

Similarly, S. Namboodiri[64] agrees with Nazrul Islam that the problem lies in lack of effective party system, and in the non-consensual approach towards identity of Bangladesh. Namboodiri believes that Bangladesh has a homogenous identiy stemming from the Bengali background. Also, within a short time it has acquired experience ranging from democratic to an authoritarian and from secular to an Islamic rule. Being largely a muslim coun-

---

63. M. Nazrul Islam, Crisis of Politics in Bangladesh, "South Asian Studies. Vol. XXIV, No. 2, July-Dec, 1989, pp. 85-93."

64. P.K.S. Namboodiri, "Bangladesh : Omnious Shadow of the Military," Strategic Analysis. Vol. VI No. 5, Aug., 1982, pp. 277-281.

try, Bangladeshis are wedded to the Islamic faith, but their cultural identity transcends r eligious dogmas. S o, t he Bangladeshi identity, he says, is a dual identity and there is confilict in Bangladeshi mind between his Bengali nationalism and his Islamic faith. Namboodiri explains that at the primary level the conflict is among three broad ideological groupings within the Bangladesh polity, which include political parties and their sympathisers and factions within the army. Three major groupings in Bangladeshi army are : (i) the revolutionary socialists, (ii) the conservatives, and (iii) the moderates - the middle roaders - all are ardent patriots to be adopted for the betterment of the Bangladesh is likely to be determined not by the civilian party politics, but by the on going ideological struggle within the army.

Dr. Golam Hussain[65], Gowher Rizvi[66], Baladas Ghoshal[67] and Iftekharuzzaman & mahabour Rahman[68] in their analysis about the role of military in the politics of Bangladesh emphasised on the lack of effective democratic institutions, lack of well organised political parties, factionalism and corruption. Under the situations of weak political institions, intra party and intra military factionalism, the suspicions made hostilities more deep and

---

65. Golam Hussain, "From Military to Military : B.N.P.'s Persistent Factionalism a nd F ailure o f C ivilian Succession i n Bangladesh" South Asian Studies Vol. XXI, No. 1, Jan-June, 1986, pp. 9-92, also see; "Military Rule in Third World Countrise," Regional Studies. Vol. IX, No. 4 Autumn, 1991, pp. 83-100.

66. Gowher Rizvi, "Riding the Tiger : Institutionalising the Military Regimes in Pakistan and Bangladesh" in Chiristopher Claphans & George Philip (eds.) The Political Dilemmas of Political Regimes (London : Gown Helm Ltd. 1985) p. 201.

corruption increased as personal interests became dominant. All these factors destablised the society and in the "praetorian" society of Bangladesh under the conditions of chaos and confusions military interventions occurred and reoccured. In the beginning military stepped into politics to aid the civil authorities, but did not go back to barracks, once it tasted power. Only environmental variables have been discussed by these writers, It may be partial truth. These writer failed to explain the nature of military establishment, its organisation, recruitment, training etc.

Zillur R. Khan[69] points that the 'aid to civil' phenomenon which occured at regular intervals after 1949 in Pakistan, whenever civil administration failed to tackle the crisis, politicised the army to a large extent. The other factors such as ideological differences within military and society, the economic crisis, the step-motherly treatment in distribution of resources and aid to military by Mujib and the creation of Rakhibahini an armed wing, by Mujib, encouraged military to play direct role in politics.

Peter J. Bertocci[70], also believes that the corruption, devasted economy, lack of institutionalisation and

---

67. Baladas Ghoshal, "Bangladesh : Passage to Military Rule" Foreign Affairs Reports. Vol. XXXI, No. 8, Aug. 1982, pp. 139-159.

68. Iftekharuzzaman and mahabudur Rehman, "Transition to Democracy in Bangladesh : Issues and Outlook," Biiss Journal, Vol. XII, No. 1, Jan, 1991, p. 95.

69. Zillur R. Khan, "Politicisation of the Bangladesh Military", Asian Survey, Vol, XXI, No. 5, May, 1981, pp. 551-564.

70. Peter J. Bertocci, "Bangladesh in the early 1980,s : Praetorian Politics in the Intermaeiate Regime" Asian Survey, Vol. XXII, No. 10, Oct, 1982, p. 988.

autocratic tendencies of Mujib led military in the political arena. Bertocci divided the society of Bangladesh in four groupings (i) the civil bureaucracy (ii) rich military (iii) the civilian politicians and (iv) rich peasent elites. Bertocci agrees with Huntington that low level of institutionalisation and high level of participation in Bangladesh has politicised military. Also, in Bangladesh, civil and military bureaucrats were more advanced than the politics between civilian and military or in mixture of relative democracy and relative dictatorships. The prevailing corruption, deteriorated economic conditions and factionalism were the causes, which culd not be eliminated by any of the regimes and thus, occured military successions one after the other.

The military succession in Bangladesh according to Razia Akhtar Bano[71] was the result of the erosion of the democratic political institutions. The political institutions could not acquire legitimacy under the absence of democratic values. Bangladesh's political institutions proved to be incapable of mediating the conflictural role among various differentiated groups of social stratas. Also, the leadership which enabled to secure independence for Bangladesh proved itself to be incapable in the task of governing the state and in turn providing an easy way for the military to play in the polity of the nation. Emphasis has been made on the political institutions only and not on military institutions by Razia Akhtar Bano.

---

71. Razia Akhtar Bano, "The Fall of Sheikh Mujib Regime : An Analysis," Indian Political Science Review Vol, XIV, No. 1 Jan, 1981, pp. 1-19.

Lawrence Lifschultz[72] has summed up the events in the life of Abu Taher which bought it to an abrupt end. He has summed up the violent and brutal political incidents. In 1975 Bangladesh entered a new phase of political upheavals. Two military putsches involving assassinations and grim jail house murders were followed by a revolutionary army mutiny. Lifschultz called it a soldiers uprising that had not been seen in the subcontinent since 1857, when the colonial army of Indian rebelled against the British. Thus the ideological orientation of military officer in Bangladesh army has been responsible for various military Juntas.

Since August 1975, the country watched one coup followed by the other. Jatiyo samajtantric Dal (J.S.D.) and Taher wanted to establish a classless army so as to give rise to a classless society and thus formulated twelve demands[73] for changing the structure of the armed forces, for release of all political prisonrers, for the armed forces, for release of all political prisonrers, for confiscation of properties of all corrupt officials and individuals, for ending all discriminbations between the officers and sepoys in armed services, for ending recruitment of officers from privileged classes, for changing the existing colonial practice, for enhancement of salary of sepoys, for abolition of the batman system, coordination and for future role of armed forces in the society for bringing revolition. Under

---

72. Lawrence Lifschultz, "Abu Taher's Last Testament, Bangladesh : The Unfinished Revolution," Economic and Political Weekly, special number, August, 1977, pp. 1303-1353.

73. For Details see : Appendix-VIII.

the conditions of political unrest zia shook hands with Taher and J.S.D. and signed the 'twelve demands' and committed himself to their implementation. After he assumed power, he realised that his personal class-based hopes and ambitions would not be materialised, if he remained under the influence of progressive forces. He ordered for the arrests of Taher and other J.S.D. leaders. He strengthened his position in military by organising special polics force. Many of the J.S.D. leaders were killed in jails and were executed. Abu Taher also faced a secret trial and was executed. The charges against Taher were mutiny and treason. Lifachultz in his article has given a detailed explanation of the testimony of secret trial[74] and of the political events which revolved round the various classes in the society and military of Bangladesh, having very narrow loyalities to their class interests and ideologies which resulted in the politics of factionalism and unfished revolution. This article contains one sided version and statement of Abu article contains one sided version and statement of Abu Taher. The objectivity of the article is questionable. Moreover, the colossal dimension of the phenomenon have many other concernable reasons aspart from the ideology which form important factors for military's intervention.

Syed Serajul Islam[75] in his analysis points that "intermediate regime" in Bangladesh gave priority to law and

---

74. For details see : Ibid. pp. 1347-1353.

75. Syed Serajul Islam, "The Rise and Installation of an Intermediate Regime in Bangladesh", South Asian Studies Vol. XXI No. 2, July-Dec 1986, pp. 51-67; also see, "The State of Bangladesh Unddr Zia (1975-81)," Asian Syrvey, Vol. XXIV, No. 5, May, 1984, p. 556.

order and thus, military became one of the powerful instruments of intermediate regime to retain power. He views military successions in Bangladesh as the result of internal contradition within the army which are affected by the external factors as well.

G.P. Deshpande[76] mentioned about the rise and fall of democratic process in Bangladesh. He is doubtful that liberal multiparty democracy in concrete terms can survive in a state in which dependent capitalism is the mainstay of power. In most such countries the fall rather than rise of democratic process has been the marked feature of the polity. Dependent capitalism needs an effective agency to maintain the law and order. Thus, G.P. Deshpande explains that military is the most viable agency to perform this task, since there is centralisation of authority in the military. But he does not take into account the cases of many developing countries which are managed by dependent capitalists and are still adhered to democratic norms.

B.K. Jahangir[77] sees military's role in politics under the changing socio-economic forces or class formations as military rules become the instrument of the dominating classes. Talukder Maniruzzaman[78], puts that urban

---

76. G.P. Deshpande, "Democracy in One Country," Economic and Political Weekly, Vol. XIX, No. 5 Nov. 10, 1984. p. 190.

77. B.K. Jahangir, "Nature of Class Struggle in Bangladesh," Economic and Political Weekly, Vol. XII, No. 5, Dec. 10, 1977, pp. 2063-66.

78. Talukder Maniruzzaman, "The Future of Bangladesh" in A. Jayaratnam Wilson & Dennis Daltons (ed.), The States of South Asia. (New Delhi : Vikas Publishing House, 1982), p. 265.

middle class came to occupy a dominating position in Bangladesh. It developed the culture of politicisation factionalism and organisations, and created hurdles for political stablity and steady economic growth. Therefore, high expectations, acute scarcity and rising prices created the atmosphere of unrest, which made army to intervene in politics several times and also tries to affect gradual disengagement of the army from politics. The writer, foresees the future of Bangladesh as characterised by political instability, slow economic growth and periodic military interventions in politics.

Shyamli Ghosh[79] tried to give different dimension for the socio-political tensions in Bangladesh. She relates the socio-political tension of Bangladesh to those of the most of the post colonial, least developed countries, which mainly relate to resource endowment and infrastructural deficiencies, social structure, nature of state power, political culture and extra societal pulls and pressures. In due to agrarian and industrial cultural subjugation and democratic and socialistic aspirations. These causes are contributary to military rule in politics but they do not explain phenomena wholly as, many democratic countries are imbibed with these problems.

Saral Patra is of the view that like many other devoloping nations the weak democratic process in Bangladesh have resulted in increased participation of armed forces in the decision-making process of the state. The war of liberation heightened the political conscious

---

79. Shymali Ghosh, "Socio-political Tensions in Bangladesh in Different Dimensions", in Kalim Bahadur (ed.), South Asia Patriot Publishers, 1986), pp, 169-177.

ness of people. Many of the armed bands of the liberation war were taken into the Bangladesh army. Such a politicised army could not remain in barracks under the deteriorating socio-economic conditions of the country. Patra says that events of the armed rule in politics of Bangladesh prove that the personnel of the Bangladesh armed forces do not constitute a class apart from the social formations they come from and are constantly influenced by the socio-economic processes that affect the people in general. That is why, whenever the democractic forces faild, the armed forces came into play the effective political role. Saral Patra has taken peculiar historycity of Bangladesh which has not been mentioned by majority of scholars.

V.P. Puchkov[81] traced the polity of Bangladesh since its independance. He has provided a good account of political and socio-economic contitions in the country at the time of independance and in different phases of civil and military rules. He has explained the advent of military regimes, their strategies and tactics to rule the country. The military interventions and coups, he belives, were the result of intense power result among different groups of the upper crust of Bangladesh society. Puchkov's analysis lack historicity, but otherwise, he has made an attempt to explain all the dimensions of the polity of Bangladesh.

Emjuddin Ahmed's[82] analytical framework is an at

---

80. Saral Patra, "Bangladesh : Martial Law regime and people" in Kalim Banadur, Ibid pp. 209-215.

81. V.P. Puchkov, Political Development of Bangladesh : 1971-1985, (New Delhi : Patriot Publishers, 1989.)

82. Emajuddin Ahamed, Military Rule and the myth of Democracy (Dhaka : University Press Ltd. 1988.)

tempt to account for the emergence of the military in Bangladesh as the ruling elite. He has taken into account the environmental factors which helped military in realising their level of organisational advantages, which motivated them to assume a political role. For explaining all these factors, Ahamed has not ignored the most important fact of politicisation of military or the armed forces which had its roots in the prindependence era. A full detail of the politics behind various coups has been given. The main emphasis is, however, on the socio-politica forces such as viz., lack of political and economic institutions, social norms and political culture, which led to military interventions in the politics of Bangladesh and helped sustain the military in power.

Borhamuddin Ahmad[83] has painted the picture of the political scenario under the authoritarian rules of the Generals of Pakistan and Bangladesh. The Generals of Bangladesh adopted the tactics of legitimisation from their predecessors. The germs of the politics deceit and jobbery, corruption, Islamisation and the gun, struck at the very roots of Pakistan and Bangladesh. He has given a good account of the events of martial laws, their brutalities and inhumanities. He has described the brute forces as the only arbiter in these counteries, their people are not mature enough to distinct between and the civil and the military. Borhanuddin Ahmad has described mainly the political strategies of the Generals. He has not emphasised much on the prevailing socio-economic or environmental conditions.

---

83. Borhamuddin Ahmad : The Generals of Pakistan and Bangladesh (New Delhi : Vikas Publishing House Pvt. Ltd. 1993.)

T.V. Sathyamurthi[84], traces out the politics of coups in Bangladesh. He also lays down the attempts of army heads to civilianise their military rule i.e. to justify the role of military in civilian affairs. He is of the view that monumental corruption of Awami League, the feckless-ness of bureaucracy at all levels, the alienation between a pro-Pakistan army and pro-India ruling party, the failure of the government to utilise the massive injections of foreign aid that it received for the purpose of laying the foundation of a producing economy and above all its ineptitude in the face of drought and famine were some of the main factors which led to military's intervention in the sphere of politics. Zia tried to civilianise his rule by following the steps of Mujib's as a leader of Awami League but Zia had to face hostilities within the military. Zia's quest for civilianisation inevitably distanced him from the armed forces which were averse to sharing of a sizeable proportion of resources. Gen. Ershad also tried to legitimise and civilianise his rule, but failed as the political bankruptcy and shallowness of the two coalitions challenged the legitimacy of his rule.

Craig Baxter[85] described 1990 as an eventful year in the history of Bangladesh as it led to the fall of Ershad and along with it military regimes which were there in the power saw their end as democratic tendencies were strengthned. Baxter called it as a new beginning for Bangladesh. Although there had been demonstrations

84. T.V. Sathyamurthi, "Betrayal of Civilian Politics", Economic and Political Weekly. Vol. XX, No. 18, May 4, 1985, p. 789.

85. Craig Baxter, "Bangladesh in 1990 : Another New Beginning," Asian Survey, Vol. XXXI, No. 2, Feb : 1991. p. 146.

against Ershad's regime since he took to power. But the popular upsurge of opposition against Ershad during November and December, 1990 swept him and his government away from office and installed a caretaker government charged with holding elections no later than March, 1991. What we can draw out from the analysis of the article is that the political parties in Bangladesh are gaining strength and they have been able to mobilise the public. The economy of Bangladesh during the two decades of military rule has not improved but only the military budget has been expanding just to make military personnel happy, as the nation is not facing any military threats. It seems that only the failures of military regime to improve the soci-economic conditions and new organisation of political parties have lead to the ouster of Gen. Ershad's military regime.

Md. Ataur Rahman[86] views that factionalism in opposition political parties and groups forces Ershad to have greater control of the political sphere. Ershad declared that "the only way to ensure stability and democracy in Bangladesh was to give a proper role to the military in our society"[87] through constitutional means. His declaration was clearly a call for the formalisation of the role expansion of the military in Bangladesh. And, he moved to expand its role by appointing a good number of military and ex-military officers to various branches of the administration. This intrusion of military in the higher echelons of the government was viewed by the bureaucracy as a threat to their basic aspirations, however, military believed

86. Md. Ataur Rahman, "Bangladesh in 1983 : A trining point for the military," Asian Survey, Vol. XXIV, No. 2 Feb. 1984, p. 240.

that the country and people needed a break from regressive bureaucrates, self-seeking and rapacious politicians. This gave rise to mutual distrust. Rahman believes that this gave rise to mutual distrust. Rahman believes that this mutual distrust was based on historical experiences as the Awami League had divided the military into freedom fighters and non-freedom fighters and also the Rakhi Bahini was created as a paramilitary force.

Most of the writers while experessing their views on the role of military in politics of Bangladesh have emphasised on the environmental factors which encouraged military to take part in politics of the country. Bangladeshi military is an over politicised military. So the internal military establishment variables have also played a role in forcing it to shoulder the internal problems of the country by participating directly into the domestic politics.

N. Mitra[88] holds that the tradition of Bangladesh's military to employ freedom fighters in army made it politicised. Mitra does not consider it a healthy apolitical tradition because this Bangladeshi tradition of politicised solider resulted in interventions in governmental sphere. Such a politically oriented military tried to seek a permanent constitutional role under the leadership of Ershad. The armed forces under the leadership of Ershad started feeling that, there is no need for them to be confined to the barracks.

---

87. Ibid, p. 243.

88. N. Mitra, "Resurrection of Zia," Strategic Analysis Vol. V, No. 9, Dec. 1981, pp. 467-471.

Sawhney[89] puts that army, as the sons of soils and as consientious citizens, the personnel should reorient themselves to the values and requirements of their newly born state. Sawhney believes that this concept is perhaps not new since many underdeveloped and developing countries are using the armed forces almost in every sphere of national life. With no visible external threat to the security of the country and since the country does not offer any attraction for the super powers in view of its geographical location, the military leadership of Bangladesh believes, that national defence and security have to be linked with political stability and economic growth. The armed forces were, thus, seeking a permanent constitutional role.

The army's intention to play a direct political role explains that military's intervention into the politics of Bangladesh was not always due to the envirnomental factors or variables, but also due to the environmental factors or variables, but also due to military's internal features. M. Choudhury[90] puts that it was only due to the internal factionalism and personal interests that military came to play role in the political sphere.

M. Choudhury examines, that the first coup in which Sheikh Mujibur Rahman was killed, was initiated by some dismissed officers on collaboration with some officers in the army. The coup was staged absolutely on personal

89. Col. R. G. Sawhney, "Bangla Army Seeks New Role," The Tribune, Chandigarh, 19 Oct., 1983. p. 4.

90. M. Chaudhury, "Military Coups and Military Rule in Bangladesh" Indian Journal of Politics, Vol. XVII, No. 34, Jan-Dec. 1983, pp. 103-111.

interests.[91] According to him it was not due to the weakness of political institutions that the military intervened in the politics of Bangladesh. The second coup was initiated by the army officers who supported Mujib's party. Khaled Mussharaf could not remain in power for more than four days because most of the army officers and soldiers supported Ziaur Rahman. The third coup which was not successful was intiated by those whose personal interests stood supreme. The last coup occured as a result of army's corporate interest and the personal interests of Ershad. Ershad as a general wanted to exercise power in Abdus Sattar's government. When Sattar resisted, Ershad took power of the government.

M. Choudhury does not agree with Huntington's view that the weakness of representative institutions is the main cause of army's intervention in politics. He argues that the coups in Bangladesh were the result of the personal interests of some dismissed army officers and of some dissatisfied soldiers in the army. The number of those who initiated the coup were quite small. However, few were able to manipulate the situation and remain in control of the government. M. Choudhury believes that the organisational characteristics of the military play a significant role in military coups. He shows that Bangladesh military is not cohesive, the army is fragmented along is succeeded by the other. Several counter-coups d' etat occured as a result of fragmentation in the army. But the role of military intervention in Bangladesh can not be explained and analysed only under this frame work. To at

91. Ibid. p. 109.

tribute the phenomenon only to the military establishment variables is the partial analysis of the problem.

K.L. Kamal[92] offered another dimension to the problem by taking Islam as a factor and pointed out that Bangladesh like Pakistan emphasised on Islamic ideology, which tended to be pro-military and excluded other ideologies from gaining ground. The implementation of reforms and imposition of laws in the name of Islam gained support and helped in consolidation of the personal power of the military rulers. Thus religion tended to sustain and legitimise the absolute power of the dictators. This was a dangerous development having far reaching consequences. The dictators in Bangladesh defined Shariat according to their own convenience. The democracy was destroyed in the name of Islam. Although Islamic ideology was adopted by the military dictators for legitimising their rule and power, only Islam can not be a factor for military's active role in politics.

Except for the works of some scholars viz., Emajuddin Ahmed, Veena Kukreja, V.P. Puchkov, most of the literature available on the role of military in Bangladesh are peacemeal in nature. Most of them are the articles in journals and news papers hence are generalistic in nature. These articles do not explain the dynamics of the problem from every angle in detail. The role of military in Bangladesh has to be perceived in the larger context. Most of the analysis are thus unidimensional.

After dealing with the existing theories and the sub-

---

92. K. L. Kamal, "The Non-Military activites of the Pakistan Military" "South Asian Studies" Vol. XVII, No. 1, Jan-June, 1982 p. 26.

ject matter available on the civil military relations in the developing nations and in the particular case of Bangladesh certain inferences can be drawn. But it is not possible to draw out one particular theory on the role of military in politics of Bangladesh as the phenomenon involves not one but innumberable facts and variables which inhibit or enhance role of military in Politics.

However, whether we classify the loss of democracy by the gravity of the phenomenon from the reduction of civil and political liberties, to temporary interruption of democratic process, to the complete displacement of democratic system or by its agent, the military or civilian executive, one thing is clear, the breakdown of democracies in Asia have not been inivitable occurences. Rather, the choices, decisions, values and actions of political and institutional leaders have figured prominently and in many cases quite clearly decisive in the decline of fall of democracy. Moreover. the decisive choices, actions and decisions have primarily been those of civilian politicians even when the military was the agent of displacing the democratic system. The objective conditions are influenced by subjective decisions and in turn subjectivity is influenced by objective conditions.

The failure of democratic systems in developing nations reveal major institutional flaws and weaknesses, which also include the failure of democratic leadership to resolve political differences and to offer stable and effective government. The military struck when democracy and legitimacy had already been eroded and the questions of identity with regard to Islam had gained importance. The military sought its role to save the nation from these problems and from rapacious and incompetent politicians.

The context of growing political polarisation, violence, indecision, government resistance and opperession provided the familiar, fertile ground for military's role in politics in Bangladesh. The analysis of developing nations provides that poverty, slow economic growth and conditions of social deprivation tend to work against democracy.

Other environmental conditions which facilitate military to intervene in politics are lack of modernisation or misdirected modernisation, low political institutionalisation, high moblisation, absence of well organised political parties and pressure groups, ideology and identity crises etc.

The fact that the military is the most modern institution in new developing countries is also true. It has the latest technology and abounds in weapons and also has a well knit cohesive and autonomous organisation. It's recruitment, training, skill structure and hierarchy in ranks provides it with a special prestige and honour. Military has adaptability and functional monopoly. Also, the societies of the developing nations feels them as most disciplined and organised force. Moreover, their ideology is more nationalistically oriented. With all such qualities it is obvious that military is a powerful and capable institution for weilding real power in any society. But what influences the role of military in politics is the all important environment within which it operates and its corresponding attachment with the civilian institutions.

In the available literature most of the scholars have highlighted one or the other dimension of the aspect and ignored the others. Some have dealt only with the organisation of military not fully dicussing the environmental factors. Even the theorists dealing with the environmental factors have not dealt with all the environmental factors, as for instance, Huntington while highlighting the political institutions ignored the culture ethos.

It is clear that one can not separate or isolate the ogranisational variables from that of environmental variables as both are complementary and supplementary to each other. It can be said, that military of the developing nations got politicised in the hands of a large number of environmental variables present in these societies, as, environment is the catalytic agent, it accelerates the process without becoming the part of the process.

In the particular case of Bangladesh, therefore, the approach to explain the role of military in politics would be a multi-dimensional one, if the particularity of the problem has to be analysed in totality. The particularity of Bangladesh lies in the historicity of the role of army in the war of liberation. So, while discussing the all important environmental variables, the notion of military establishment in Bangladesh is also important to analyse. It is thus, important to cover all the aspects suggested by the literature reviewed above.

The modus operandi of phenomenon has a circular causation having cumulative effect. The relative importance of variable depends upon the contextuality and historicity which trigger the military to intervenne in politics.

III-Historical Perspective

The changes that take place in the polity of a nation can not be explained or analysed without particularity of the area under investigation. History has its own significance. Events do not only step in deliberate polices but are also conditioned by past habits and traditions. Thus, history assumes a sole linkage between present and past. It helps in formulating analytical framework for the understanding of political phenomenon without dealing with the historical perspective. Therefore, there is dire necessity to go through the historicity of the problem.

Bangladesh, though a newly independent nation state, is a very ancient land. The earlier references of it are found as early as sixth century B.C. in the Aitarey Arayanke.[1] In it, the territory neighbouring Magadha on the East is identifies as Banga. The king of Banga was supposed to have fought in the battle of Kurukshetra in the camp of Duryodhana. The Mahabharat actually specifies the names of two kings-Chitrasen and Samudrasen. Together with Harivamsa, it describes the land east of the Bhagirathi river as Banga. This is also confirmed by Kalida in his Raghuvansa. In the seventh century A.D. a king named Deva

1. Subrata Banerjee, Bangladesh, (New Delhi : National book trust, 1981). p.2.

Kharga was known to be the ruler of Banga.

References of land Banga the East of Bhagirathi have been found in many medieval copper plate inscriptions.[2] It was during the Pathan rule that the entire territory, came to be known as Bengal. From eleventh century onwards Bengal was brought under one centrialised authority-under the Mughals, the political bundaries of the territory were further extended. Mughal rule was however, confined to towns. The country side remained in the hands of dispossessed Afghan nobles and Chieftains. The whole of Bengal was a territory under military control and not an integral part of the colonial empire's administration. Such a situation naturally led to suppression on one hand spirt of rebelion on the other. These two features can be felt even in today's Bangladeshi society, seeds of "praetorianism" go to back to this period.

The history of East Bengal is mainly the history of a struggle for autonomy. This is consistent with the most significant trend in the history of Bengal since the conquest of the land by Mohammad Khilji at the close of the twelth century. "The muslim governors of Bengal defied the authority of the muslim sovereigns of Delhi, rebelled against them and often ruled as independent kings."[3]

Fakhrudin's revolt against the tyranny of Mohammad-bin-Tughlak virtually separated Bengal from the Delhi sultanate in 1340 and the imperial rule of the provinces was not restored till 1526, when Akbar's general defeated

2. Ibid.

3. R.K. Dasgupta, Revolt in East Bengal (New Delhi : Navana Printing works, Pvt. Ltd., 1971), p. 52.

4. Ibid p. 53.

Daudshah.[4] Thus, Bengali identity can be traced from the ancient period. Coming of Pathan and Muslim rulers added religious dimension to Bengali identity. The question of identity has not been solved till today.

The politically awakened Bengali, be he a Hindu or a Muslim, remained allergic to a central authority located a thousand miles away, whether that authority was Pathan or Mughal or whether it was British of Pakistan later on.

Muslim rule cracked vertically and horizontally the homogenous Bengali identity. Muslim rule created intellectual elite i.e., 'Alam', the Arabic scholars. The governing elite consisted of the officials like Kazi; the judge; the priestly elite, the mullah; and the spirtitual elite, the fakirs; amongst whom were the pirs and Murshids, who had a very large popular following. Apart from professional classes, there were the classes based on race and descent i.e. the syeds, the descendents of Mohammad's grandson through his daughter; the Sheikhs, the muslim of Arab origin; the Pathans, the muslim of Afghan origin and the Moghals, who came from Central Asia. Thus, Asharaf / Azalaf cleavages are by product of pathan and muslim rules.

The large number of muslims of Bengal were mainly the descendents of Hindus, converted into Islam. After the Mulsim conquest of Bengal in the thirteenth century majority of muslims of Bengal were low caste hindus who were converted into Islam. Thus, Bengali Muslim culture was a blend of Hinduism and Islam. The Bengali Muslim culture was, thus, more tolerant to Hinduism than that of West Pakistan.

Before the advent of British rule, Bengal plays a significant role in trade and commerce. "Ninety five varieties of cotton silk and mixed pieces goods, were exported from Bengal presidency alone to various parts of the world, other kinds of fabrics consumed locally in the early nineteenth century."[5] "No part of India possessed such natural advantages, both for agriculture and commerce."

The Mughal did not have a permanent national army, the bulk of the army consisted of irregular forcess, which were raised and maintained by local chieftains. Thus, the irregular armed forces could be raised in hour of need under different conditions and situations. The present non-corporate identity of army has its roots in the history.

The battle of Plassey of 1757 gave first blow to muslim rule in Bengal. After that, rest of India was seized by the Britishers. Underdevelopment in Bengal started when British mercantile bourgeoisie monopolised all important trades of Bengal. It started extracting from Indian producers as much as possible and gave them in return virtually nothing. Britishers pursued a policy of plundering by looting away resources of Bengal. Lord Macaulay writes that, "after the battle of Plassey, the shower of wealth fell on the company and its servants. A sum of eight hundred thousand sterling, in coined silver was sent down the river form Murshidabad to Fort William (later Calcutta). The fleet which conveyed this treasure consisted of more than hundred boats...the treasury of Bengal was thrown open to Clive, who walked between heaps of gold and silver, crowned with rubies and diamonds and was at liberty

---

5. B.N. Ganguly quoted in M. Sayefullah Bhuiyan, "Underdevelopment of Bangladesh; An Analysis of Socio-economic Policy Implications," South Asian Studies. Vol. XXIX, No. 2, July-Dec. 1989. p. 29.

6. Lord Macaulay outed in Ibid.

to help himself."[7]

The disastrous socio-economic policies followed by British brought extereme poverty for the masses of Bengal. The poverty grew as the British rule progressed. The nature of exploitation was crude, archaic and uncivilised. After 1857, it took industrial character with the creation of civil and military bureaucracy and an efficient police force To satisfy the greed for land revenue and to ensure its collection in time, the British gave rise to a body of rich landed zamindars who had good relations with the Britishers and had a complete control over masses. Such bureacuratic and feudal elements who had western education gave rise to a distinct class. There was not such of a difference between these elements and their colonial masters.

Major socio-economic changes took place in Bengal under Britishers. There was a new turn in the social history of Bengal after the Battle of Plassey, particularly after the permanent settlement of 1793. The new revenue system introduced by Lord Cornwallis ruined the muslim aristocracy in Bengal, prevented the growth of the muslim middle class and on the whole diminished the status of Bengali muslim in society and state.[8] In the past, Muslims monopolised the police and the army, and held most of the posts of revenue and judicial officers.

---

7. Quoted in M. Sayefullah Bhuiyan, Op. cit. p. 30.

8. Gilbert Etienne, Bangladesh : Development in Perspective, (Delhi : The Macmillan Company of India Limited, 1979) p. 7.

In Bengal, the overwhelming majority of muslims, who were mainly peasants, now came under the Hindu landlords. The Britishers tried to imbibe the class consciousness and communal feeling among the muslims masses. These characteristics are visible even today. Thus, Britisher's policy of divide and rule created a gap between two communities and paved the way for non-secular political institutions.

It was in Bengal that the first spark of revolt was ignited. The revolt gradually spread to the whole of Eastern India. But Bengal remained the main centre. Immediately after 1857, Peasants of Bengal participated wholeheartedly in the indigo revolt. "It is important to note that at least seventeen out of thirty four armed peasant uprisings in Bengal, in the span of 136 years were concentrated and even originated in Bengal."[9] The exploitation of masses at the hands of rulers or the landlords, has, thus, always resulted in direct action of people with the help of arms, in the history of Bangladesh. Thus, the feature of political unrest in Bengali society is a historical legacy.

The sons of new landlord families took English education and government employment, gave rise to the Hindu Bengali urban middle class. It was in this class, that the ideas of nationalism and democracy first germinated towards the end of the nineteenth century. Whereas muslim community discarded British education and confined themselves to "Madarsa" system and remained devoid of liberal education. The muslim class, had not been able to acquire the nationalistic, democratic norms, which later

---

9. Subrata Banerjee, Op. cit. p. 34.

on resulted in giving rise to authoritarianism and non-secularism.

As the new Hindu educated class started emerging, it became aware of the tactics of Britishers. This class came up as a threat to the British rulers. The Britishers started sympathising with the muslims. The muslim elites too realised the need to cooperate with the Britishers started aympathising with the muslims. The muslim elites too realised the need to cooperate with the Britishers to avoid the domination of Hindus. The Britishers recruited Muslims at various places, manily in police and jail services and used them against nationalists, the majority of whom Hindus. By this policy the question of common nationality was thwarted. Britishers sowed the seeds of communalism by counter- poising one community against the other, and gave religious dimension to the Bengali identity. They uprooted the secular ethos and throttled mass commercialisation.

The people of Bengal had a marked political consciousness. Rashtraguru Surenderanath Banerjee founded Indian Association in 1876.[10] This was immediately followed by the foundation of Central National Mohammedan Association (CNMA) by a muslim leader of Bengal in 1877.[11] C.N.M.A. presented a memorandum to British government in order to seek nrmedies of their grievances.

The muslims of Bengal like the muslims of ther parts of India favoured the British attitude of the division of Bengal in 1905 as they thought that it was in favour of

---

10. D.N. Benerjee, East Pakistan : A Case Study in Muslim Politics (Delhi : Vikas Publications, 1969) p. 22.

11. Ibid.

their own economic and political interests. But, the British purpose behind division was to weaken the the Indian National Congress by dividing Bengal. The objective was sought to be achieved by setting one community against another.

In order to enhance their interests, the Bengali muslims felt the need for an organisation. The British government also preferred a muslim political organisation as a counter weight against the growing strength of the Indian National Congress. Therefore, in 1906, under the initiation of nawabs of Dhaka, Muslim League was founded in Dhaka. This was a non-secular institution, having negative connotation, which lateon resulted in authoritarianism.

By 1909, Muslim League managed to achieve separate representation taking into account both their proporation of the population and the community's political importance. A muslim idenity has been established in Indian politics, whose programme was more of a negative one, i.e. it was committed to the safeguarding of the interestes of a section of the society, which at that time were muslims. Thus, political institutions were negative in character which inhibited democratic consciousness and gave rise to non-secular ethos.

Though, Fazlul Huq never believed in the two nation theory, he knew that Bengal's problem was fundamentally economic and required some radical solution under the democratic institutions. He extended his hand of friendship to Congress in order to solve the Hindu-Muslim problem of Bengal but all India leadership of Congress had other ideas and did not allow its Bengal Provincial branch to accept the invitation of Huq and the oppertunity to solve the communal problem of Bengal in order to establish a secular and democratic base was lost. On the other hand Jinnah lost no time in bringing Huq and his following to the fold of Muslim League. So, non-secular politics were allowed to have their way in the politics of Bengal. Also, the Muslim middle class of Bengal felt that the only way to get rid of the Hindu domination was to make Bengal a part of a muslim homeland. They, therefore, decided to support the Muslim League, and in the early forties, induced the poor Muslims to join the same organisation in large numbers.[12]

Gunnar Myrdal says, the authoritarian personality of Jinnah ran the league like a General issuing orders to his troops and local commanders.[13] The tendency of lack of plurality of leadership and democratic debates remained in the East Bengali politics even after independence of Bangladesh.

The upshoot that was nurtured by the supra Bengal course of alienation in Indian society, the region and religion wise alienation of Bengali people won over their ethnic and national identity. Nation-building and state formation in Bengal took an unprecedented turn. In 1947, Bengal went under two state formations ; West Bengal to the Indian Union and East Bengal to Pakistan.

The administrative system that was built in British

---

12. Ram Krishna Mukherjee, "Nation Building and State Formation in Bangladesh" in S.P. Verma & Virender Narain (eds.), Pakistan Political System in Crisis. (Jaipur : South Asia Studies Centre, University of Rajasthan, 1972). pp. 151-153.

13. Gunnar Myrdal, Asian Drama, Vol. I, (New Delhi : Kalyani Publishers, 1982), p. 311.

India, was primarily extractive in nature and this was in effect the chief instrument of control and domination. The administrative system was organised to meet the specific needs of the British rule. The government was build on the concept of authority. "The image of colonial administration", says William Boyer, "as a high and haughty platonic guardian or mandrain, keeping order and performing routine services by deploying instruments of authority toward a passive and compliant public, from whom he maintains an appropriate social distance, now appears archaic and antithetical to development administration."[14]

During the first colonial period, in British regime, the experimentation of local government was more on rural administration than on local government. The reason was obvious, in the first phase of colonial rule, articulation of power between the village and the colonial rule, articulation of power between the village and the colonial administration was mediated by the Panchayats or Union Committees in which appointment of the members were made by the administration. The members were the traditional power holders of the village, normally from the leading land lord families. They were holders of quasi-political office, they were nediator between the administration and the rural areas and this way local power was assimilated into the political system of the raj through the administration.

After the enactment of 1919 (village self governemnt act) there was a shift in the rural level power. political

---

14. William W. Boyer, A Report on Development Administration in Bangladesh. (Dacca : Asia Foundation, April 1975), typed script, p.3

parties entered energetically into the arena of national-political parties and established ties with rural faction leaders. In the articulation of power, a new channel was established between the rural faction leaders and the politicians at urban level. This Channel was in operation parallelly with the older channel between the rural notables and the colonial administration. The scope and powers of representative bodies were gradually expanded untill, under the 1935 Indian Act[15], the provinces were governed by cabinets nominated by the state assemblies, most of whose members had been elected by locals on a greatly expanded but still restricted franchise. An elected national assembly was also established under the 1935 act, but with much more limited powers than the state assemblies and no effective controls over the central government headed by the governor-general appointed by London.

The basic operating principles of a highly authoritarian martial law regime were defined in precise legal terms by the British and imposed on the raj in 1939-45 period. Thus, When Pakistan military first moved into the uncertain world of a martial law regime in 1958 and Bangladeshi military in 1975, they could refer back to the extebsuve British experience with such a system in the subcontinent during world war-II.

The establishment of British political power in india brought some order to the disarranged military condition in the country. They did not bring a large army for their protection and recruited soldiers from the local folks. For administrative and military purposes the whole country

15. Ibid p.8

was put under three divisions-Bombay, Bengal and Madras.[16] The Bengal Presidential army was of mised classes. Under the military code of 1807 Britishers started recruitment on caste basis. During the period of 1820's the recruitment of the people on high caste orign went on rapidly in all three presidency armies and more of less wholly in the Bengal army. Thus, Bengal army inherited class and communal consciousness right from its inception. The basis of recruitment were more or less ascribed. The army lacked tradition of professionalism.

Bengal armies arose from the preponderance of high caste recruits and an unforutante serving of paternalised tie which linked sepoys with their British officers. Bengal recruits fitted nearly into all the categories of soldierly like appearance that had been devised in Britain. Bengal sepoys were drawn from agrarian society, which were cosidered as, a sturdy independent peasantry by the english-roughly equivalent to the idealised scottish highlander. The dominance of higher caste in Bengal army was reinforced even by the sepoys themselves, taking charge of recruitment, when they returned to the regiment from furloughs, they brought family and kin members back with them as prospective recruits. This in times of extraordinary demand the army actively sought recruits itself. By 1920, the army of Bengal had its own characteristic recruits being only from higher castes. This was further refined by narrow regional focus as Brahmins and Rajputs

---

16. For Detail see : Doughlas, M. Pears, "The Habitual Nobility of Being : British officers and the Social Construction of the Bengal Army in the Early Nineteenth Century," Modern Asian Studies, Vol. XXV, Part 3, July, 1991, pp. 565-566.

from Awadh and neighbouring areas of Bihar and Rohilkhand made up most of the Bengal army.

The Burmese war brought natural inferiority to the sepoys of Bengal. The troops from Madras were coneidered to be on foreign service and were, therefore, paid extra. The discontent within the army eventually culminated in Barrackpore mutiny. Thus, mutinies are historical legacies of Bengali soldiers. Most of the British officers started unrelying the Bengal army. As a result, Whereas by1815 sixty percent of all officers were Bengali in the regiments, by 1830 this figure was halved.[17]

During the middle period of the nineteenth century the conditions in the army were not so favourable for the uppercaste men. Within the army it became impossible to play simultaneously the role of a civilian high caste man, observe the caste discipline and that of a military man and observe the military discipline. These two roles came into conflict in the army and fumes of discontent spread among the high caste men. This feeling intensified because of the westernising and Christianising policy of the government, and in 1857, issue of cartridges was obnoxious to high caste Hindus and Mulsims, which sparked off the great mutiny. The mutiny flared up only in the Bengal army, the madras and Bombay armies with a few exceptions remained loyal to the government.[18] In Bengal army, the sepoys were able to organise the mutiny well, as most of the regiments consisted men of one caste and one region, who were carried away by the primary group loyalities and regional affiliations. There was a feeling of oneness among

17. Ibid, p. 567.
18. Ibid, p. 568.

the sepoys and they acted as if they were members of one family.

British Indian army based on religious, linguist and regional affiliations was trained in the interest of the imperial rulers, their policies had been devised to capitablise on the existing religious antagonisms between the religious minorities through its policy of 'divide and rule' For the maximum utilisation of the Indian military element the deployment strategy was based on the following dictum : "keep against Hindoos, keep your Hindoos out of the Punjab, and they will be ready to act against Sikhs."[19]

After the mutiny of 1857, various low caste members were taken into the military. A large number of people had been taken from hilly areas and the North-west Frontier areas (N.W.F.A.), They were recruited to suppress the revolt. Towards the middle of the eighteen seventies the recruitment started taking place on the basis of the certain regional units, as a result large number of recruitment took place from areas of Punjab and N.W.F.A. consisting of Sikhs, the Mohamadans, the Hindu Dogras and the Jats.

Later, the base of recruitment became confined to the martial races, as such groups were rough and tough and could bear arms in any type of conditions. By this, the government had an idea that only the people who came from north and north western regions of Indian could possess that martial spirit to fight. At least for four decades the martial races and classes instead of castes became the catchword in the army.

---

19. C. H. Philip, The Evolution of India and Pakistan (London : oxford University press, 1962), p. 508.

Under the new recruitment grounde the army got a new composition, which excluded 'nationalist' and partlcularly 'volatile' Bengalis. The Ratio between British and Indian elements in army also underwent a change. This was designed to strengthen surveillance of the 'native' troops by the British officers.

"Prior to 1857 there were 40,000 British troops in an army of 3,00,000. In 1867, the number of British troops as raised to 61,747. The ratio of approximately one to two between the British and Indian elements was viewed nacessary for the colonial government's objective of maintaining law and order and ensuring internal security. At a time when British troops were not willing to join the British Indian Army in larger numbers, it was decided to decrease the size of the army to 120,000 in 1867 with a view to maintaining the ratio. In 1878, the strength of the British Indian Army stood at 189,597, with 6002 British officers, 60,341 British and 123,254 Indian soldiers."[20]

Apart from surveillance arrangement the Indian troops in the British Indian Army were indocrinated in such a fashion that they ultimately became alienated from the mainstream of national political activities and national culture. One of the main principles of development strategy for the Indian troops was such that, "they shall be deprived, as far as possible, of community and national sentiment and interest, and be recruited and constituted as to act in time of excitement and disturbance, as a check upon the other."[21]

"Among the military officers in British India, the as

20. Ibid, p. 513.
21. Ibid, p. 515.

similation displayed itself not merely in the exquisitely tailored lounge suits of officers in mufit, in a panchant for understatement, for beautiful silver and for cavalry moustaches but also in their belief that politicians were no more than "Scallywags"[22] Maj. Gen Fazal Muquren Khan noted that in British India the life of a military officer was deeply influenced by the examples of the British officers. He worte, "His reading habits were also formed in their society and he would read the same books from the same club library. Perhaps he began his day with the "London times" read 'Punch' at lunch and went to bed with the 'London Illustrated News' or 'The Tatler', The delay in the arrival of the 'Blackwood magazine' worried him as much as it would any British officers."[23] Thus, military had the characteristic of Britishers life style they developed distrust to politicians and worked against their polies.

"In British India, military service came to be equated with honour and also with land, as the British took over the ancient tradition of the Jagir or land grant for loyal military service."[24] After the World war-I the soldiers were granted land in Punjab i.e. north and north-west areas and as the Britishers continued their recruitment policy based in martial races, most of the military services were drawn from these areas. Thus, the element of prestige,

---

22. Emajuddin Ahamed, Military Role and the myth of Democracy, (Dhaka : University Press Ltd., 1989). p. 34.

23. Quoted in Ibid.

24. Hugh Tinker, India and Pakistan : A Political Analysis, (London : Pall Mall Press, 1962), p. 154.

economic security and honour was present inthe military services in colonial period. This colonial legacy is still prevalent in the Bangladesh military.

The esablishment of British Indian Army was based on the supremacy of British officers and the subordination of Indian soldiers. The regid hierarchy strongly rejected any possibility of promotion from the lower ranks. However, the competitive spirit was sustained by creating a layer of N.C.O's (Non-Commissioned Officers), subordinate to the officer corps, and the liaison man between officers and men. "Both the NCO's and the soldiers were encouraged to regard themselves as superior to their fellow citizens, and to believe that they It was only after 1918 that the Indians were allowed into the officer corps, but such selected officers were drawn exclusively from landed families, whose reliability was beyond doubt. Such a nexus among the landed elite, military and bureaucracy could be later felt in Pakistan army as well as in bangladesh's army. These officers were modelled on their British superiors in everyway. Such ethos became integral parts of the training at R.M.A. (Royal Military Academy) Sandhurst and later in I.M.A. (Indian Military Academy) Dehradun and Kakul Military Academy in Pakistan."

The regional concentration within the so called martial races continued in the army. In 1929, 54% of total combatant troops in the Indian army were supplied by Punjab.[26] And almost all of them came from rural landowing areas as the Britishers considered them to be

25. Tariq Ali, Pakistan : Military Rule of People's Power. (New York : William Morrow & Company, 1970), p. 64.

better fighters and the urban educated class were considered to be efficient for clerial works.

The Policies which were followed by British Indian Army were actually laid down by the civil government in London. It performed four major functions. First, to check the intrusion of foreign traders in Indian territory, Secondly, to establish law and order, thirdly, to assist the civil government in India and fourthly, the Indian troops were used in British government's military expeditions. All these helped the Indian military to achieve an outstanding position. They also came closer to the political sphere of action.

However, the British recruitment policy based on martial races had no r oom for politically awakened Bengalis. "Bengal with a population of 45 million, provided 700 combatant recruits, the Punjab with a population of 20 millions provided 349,000 such recruits. The Punjab and the united provinces between them provided three fourth of the total number of combatant recruits raised through out India."[28]

After the birth of Pakistan, apart from communalism, the regional and linguistic dimensions were added in the Bengali politics and there was great resentment among Bengali army personnel.

---

26. Bilal Hashmi, "Dragon Seed : Military in the State," in Hasan Gardezi and Jamil Rashid (ed.), Pakistan : The Roots of Dictatorship : the political economy of Practorian State, (Delhi : Oxford University Press, 1983), p. 152.

27. See Hasan Askari Rizvi, The Military and Politics in Pakistan 1947-86. (New Delhi : Konark publishers, 1988), pp. 14-16.

28. Quoted in Emajuddin Ahamed, op. cit, p. 38.

Pakistan came into existence on 14th August, 1947, with Eastern and western zones, "while its western zone was dry, the eastern one was sheet of water. The former was rugged and relatively empty and the later desperately over populated. Their culture and outlook were radically divergent. The eastern zone had higher literacy rate than western. The economic structure was totally different."[29] So the people of the two wings had antithetical characters. The fatal flaw in yoking these two wings separate from each other resulted in the inevitable crisis and military interventions which disintegrated Pakistan.

Table-1

Demographic Data of the Two Wings :[30]

S.No.	Pakistan	East Pakistan	West Pakistan
1. Area (sq. miles)	3,65,529	55,126	3,10,403
2. Population:			
(a) 1961 census (000)	93,720	50,804	42,880
% increase in 1951-61	23.9	21.2	27.1
(b) Persons per Sq. mile	256	922	138
(c) Literates (000)	14,336	8,956	5,380
% of population	23.9	17.6	13.6
(d) Rural population (%)	86.9	94.8	77.5
3. Land Utilisation in 1965-66			
(a) Total area (m. acres)	233.9	35.3	198.6
(b) Not reported (m. acres)	68.0	nil	68.0

(c) Forest (in %)	10.3	5.4	4.9
(d) Not available for cultivation (in %)	53.1	6.3	46.8
(e) Other cultivated (in %)	32.8	1.3	31.5
(f) Cultivated area (in %)	13.4	0.7	12.7

At the time of independence East Bengal had a political and economic structure that was radically different from that of the west Pakistan provinces. The wealthiest strata of Pakistani society lived in West Pakistan, it was they who dominated the Muslim league, the army and the bureaucracy. As after partition most of the highclass Hindus migrated to India. "With regard to administration, the departure of many Hindus of I.C.S., who opted for Pakisatan, there were only two Bengalis,"[31] In fact, in between the rural masses and politicians, there was only a very thin layer of cadres in any field of activity. Natural calamities and lack of flood controls deteriorated the socioeconomic condition of East Pakistan. The break down of administrative institutions inhibited democratic growth.

The large scale migration of Hindus belonging to landowning, professionals, commercial-industrial classes, leas

29. N.N. Gidwani, "Genesis and Growth of Pakistan" in S.P. Verma and Virender Narain (ed.) Pakistan Political System in Crisis : Emergence of Bangladesh. (Jaipur : South Asian Studies Centre, 1972), p. 11.

30. "Bangladesh Basic Facts reported in International Conference on Bangladesh in New Delhi, (Published by Radha Krishna, 1971), p. 38.

31. Gilbert Etienne, op, cit, p. 31.

to a big gap in the social and economic structure of East Pakistan. In fact, the migration of the Hindu Zamindars, money lenders and professional people from East Bengal led to the rise of the new higher and middle classes in East Bengal and ultimately paved the way for "Praetorianism."

The West Pakistan's social structure reflected semifeudal and tribal class. It inherited over-repesented colonial state structures, like civil and military bureaucracy, the political institutions like political parties and pressure groups, remained under-developed. Whereas, East Pakistan had a different situation, wealthy land owning class ceased to exist, under such vacuum, a social structure emerged which came to be dominated by a mass of peasants, small land holders and professional middle classes.

Pakistan followed a capitalist development policy which served the dominant class interests of Pakistan. The socio-economic policies of Pakistan were framed and implemented by the bureaucracy, which had extensive powers. The bureaucratic decisions and investment power directly favoured the West Pakistani bourgeoisie who managed to accumulate enormous wealth. Bengalis had almost no participation in the decision making process.

The Bengali muslims gradually felt the need for spelling out their ideas on their culture and social values. They realized that to fulfil their political aspirations, They must first accomplish a cultural renaissance to sustain their new sense of nationhood.

Right since the inception of Pakistan, The people of East Bengal were constantly subjected to economic and socio-cultural exploitation reminiscent of the traditional relationship between an imperial power and a colony.

During the period 1947-1954 the Bangladesh nationalist movement took the form of a language question. In the period 1954 to 1965 this movement emphasised on the federal balance and regional autonomy for East Bengal. The identity and legitimacy to military rule discrediting the political institutions and political parties.

The first martial Law in the country was imposed on 6th March, 1953, and "gave the people of Lahore and Pakistani army an opportunity to see what would be accomplished by strong and speedy measures."[32] This temporaty peace and order restored by the army raised their esteem in the public eye and discredited the politicians even further.

After the 1954 elections, on April 3, 1954 A.K. Fazlul Huq formed the United Front ministry. He offered cooperation to Karachi, but conditioned this to the fulfilment of demands on the issues of language, constitution and provincial autonomy for the province, was perceived by the civilmilitary oligarchy at the cnetre as the beginning of the crumbling of their bastion of power. Governor rule was clamped on East Pakistan and a proposal for the integration of the four provinces of the West Pakistan into 'One Unit' was mooted in the constituent assembly,[33] so that the Bengalis would he unable to exploit the differences between the West Pakistani provinces. The showdown that ensued, saw the dramatic dissolution of the constituent assembly and the creation of the new ministry of

---

32. Khalid Bin Sayeed, Pakistan : The Formative Phase (Karachi : Pakistan Publishing House, 1960), p. 71.

33. Ibid, p. 72.

all talents, including General Ayub Khan, Commander-in-Chief of armed forces as defence minister and Iskander Mirza, a civil-servant as minister of the interior. The new constitent assembly was called and the constitution of Pakistan was finally adopted in 1956. The non-consensual constitution was prepared and adopted by unrepresentative elites which effectively nipped the democratic process in bud in Pakistan.

The socio-econimic conditions were equally responsible for increasing frustration and alienation in Pakistan society. As a result, the experiment of Parliamentary democracy in Pakistan was a fiasco. The attitude of East Bengalis in the latter half of 1950s was one of frustration. With the frustration in the minds and attitudes, the East Bengalis were moving towards an authoritarian system under the Pakistani rule.

"Whenever, the bureaucratic set up felt that its power and privileges were being threatned either by the legislature or by other socio-political forces operating within the country, it would either dismiss the legislature or split the political parties or play one politican against the other. This powerful clique in the bureaucracy did not allow democracy to take roots in the country and so manoeuvred the levels of political power in their hands as to discredit whatever democratic institutions were still functioning. In order to realise the ambition of power, The bureaucratic clique reduced democratic institutions to a farce."[34]

The bureaucracy, in close consort with the army dominated politics in Pakistan throughout but with a mask provided by chosen politicians till 1958, when the army in

34. Ibid, p. 78.

stead of remaining a back seat driver, chose itself to manoeuvre the steering wheel. It is interessting to note that the bureaucratic clique in Pakistan with the help of political stooges did hammer out a constitution in 1956 which gave enormous power to president. "political ambitions of Pakistan's bureaucracy were so overwhelming that whenever political process, such as elections were allowed to take place, they were reduced to a farce. Such gross interferences proved fatal for the democratic politics of the country."

President Mirza staged a coup in October, 1958, dismissed the cabinet and held the confidence of the national assembly, suspended the constitution and imposed martial law with full backing of Ayub Khan. After the promulgation of Martial Law in 1958 and assumption of presidentship of Ayub Khan, army became the steering wheel of political power and remained dependent on bureaucracy, The development of the civil-military clique led to the demise of parliamentary democratic institutions. Under Ayub's regime the two main sources of authority remained, the institutions of civil service and the army. The demand for autonomy of Bengali's inherent in the very fabric of Pakistani state became substantial during Ayub regime. Through the institutions of 'Basic Democracy' Ayub further consolidated the grip of centralised-military-industrial elite over East Pakistan. Military intervened mainly due to lack of effecitve democratic institutions, mass based political parties and organised pressure groups.

Ayub's "Basic Democracy" Shifted power to the rural elite, away from urban centres. The most unique, non-evolutionary easpect of 'Basic democracies' was the use of local councils to alter the basic formulae by which the state was governed. Ayub used the Basic democrats as an electoral college to choose the head of state and the national and provincial assemblies. This had the effect of politically decapitating the urban centres and institutionalising rural notables as important actors in the national arena."[35] The interdependence of administration and village authority intertwined economy and role of authority in rural areas. Ayub's experimentation brought a change in the mode of articulation of power of the rural areas with the national polity and made it instead of two parallel power currents, a central power current from now on subordinate only to the interests of the political administration. At the rural level economic power became a significant factor in the consolidation of authority position. These authority position holders made various alliances to control village and intervillage power politics. "In this system economic dependence and kinship allegiance were used as strategies in dealing with other faction leaders in the same plane and with the higher faction leaders on a different plane."[36] This way in place of class politics, politics of oppurtunism started and the participation of the faction leaders into the politics of competition generated not only factional in party politics but party system was deteriorated to a great extent. Thus, at the

---

35. E. L. Tepper, "The Administration of Rural Reform : Structural constraints and Political Dimensions," in Hamza Alvi and peter Bertocci (ed.) Rural Development in Bangladesh and Pakistan (Honolulu : University of Hawaii press, 1966), p. 49.

36. B.K. Jahangir, "Social Organisation, Process and Change in Bangladesh", The Journal of Social Sturies, No. 14, Oct. 1981, p. 30.

level of legislative institutions the members of the vested interests proliferated. The, 'Basic democracy' was used to control the people without dislodging the rich peasants from the power base of rural establishment. This was to make rural powerholders as clients of the ruling political elites. During this period the role of political parties was reduced to minimal and democratic tradition could not develop. Thus, the inatitutions of interst aggregation and social mobilisation could not gain ground.

In the absence of democratic political institutions, the atrocities of Ayub Khan regime on East Bangalis' continued. At such a stage Mujibur Rahman came forward with his 'six point programme' which he issued on March 23, 1966. "The six point programme provided the basic principles of a firm solution to the country's inter-wing political and economic problems."[37] This programme found a great popular support in East-Pakistan. The resulting unrest in the country provided for the military to play its role in aid to civil functions. Whenever there was indication that East Bengal had the power or resources to over throw the ruling of military elites of West Pakistan, the moves were crushed ruthlessly.

During Pakistan period civil services came to acquire important position in the sphere of politics and created military-bureaucratic supremacy. This clique rendered democratic institutions ineffective. The system of basic democracies for rural development expanded the bureaucratic control. The military-bureaucratic role in the politics of the country furthered the socio-economic disparties

---

37. S.K. Chakravarty, The Evolution of Politics in Bangladesh : 1947-78. (New Delhi : Associated Publishing House, 1978)p. 135.

between the two wings of Pakistan. Moreover, the military regime was most opposed in East Pakistan and not in West Pakistan as most of the bureaucratic and military elites were from West Pakistan.

After military takeover in 1958, the Bengali language and culture was looked down upen and restoration of Bengali culture was met with ruthlessness. The economic conditions of East Pakistan went on deteriorating. The transfer of resources from agriculture to industry involved the re-distribution of income favour of a rich 'saver class' and in favour of West Pakistan. The Gross National Product (G.N.P.) of East Pakistan was 86 percent of G.N.P. of Pakistan in 1949-50. By 1967-68 it was around 65%[38]. The rate of growth per capita income in East Pakistan was lower than in west pakistan. In some years, the rate of growth in East Pakistan was negative. Furthermore, the structural change that took palce in Pakistan was more pronounced in the Western wing. The patterns of saving, investment and trade were also quite different in the two wings. A considerable trade diversion occured in both wings of Pakistan. "Over the period 1950-65, East Pakistan had a defficit on her account with West Pakistan and a surplus with the rest of the world. In contrast, West Pakistan had a large and growing deficit with the rest of the world and a surplus on her account with East Pakistan. Over the period as a whole East Pakistan had an overall trade defficit

---

38. Javed Ansari and Mary Kaldor, "Military Technology and Conflict Dynamic : The Bangaldesh Crisis in 1971" in Mary Kaldor and Asbjorn Eide (eds.) The World Military order : The Impact of Military Technology on the third world, (London : The Macmillan Press Ltd., 1979) pp. 39-40.

of Rs. 4 Crores (40m) per annum compared with Rs. 70 crores per annum for West Pakistan; upto 1960, East Pakistan had a surplus on its overall trade balance."[39]

The government of Pakistan did a little to check the growing regional disparity. Quite the contrary, its economic policy acentuated the disparity mainly through the transfer of resources from agriculture to industry. Thus, The East Pakistani society faced a continuous discrimination at the hands of military rulers of West Pakistanm which had serious impact on national integration. The then East Pakistanis were excluded from the decision and policy making process and this gave rise to Bengali subnationalism and finally to a movement for a separate state for Bangladesh.

The people of Bengal realised that in trying to escape the Hindus of Bengal, they had fallen under the domination of West Pakistan. The Bengali middle-class-The professionals, the bureaucrats, military officers, the small traders found their illusions shattered.

When the Bengalis arose for cultural self determination, they fought against the concept of religion as the basic nationhood. They now distinguished between Islam as a religion and Islam as a political force. "Rejection of Islam as a political concept, no longer meant rejection of Islam as a religion."[40] In the past they had opposed their muslim culture to the culture of the Bengali Hindus, now they opposed their Bengali culture to the culture of West Pakistan. In the past their muslim culture was only a weapon in their hands, now their Bengali culture was a

39. Ibid., p. 141.

40. Subrata Banerjee, Op.cit., p. 50.

thing of their soul. Their Bengali language soon became the very symbol of their cultural identity and they soon realised that they could save that identity only by saving the prestige of their language and culture. The imposition of Urdu became the main cause of discontent in East Bengal.

The language difference caused dispute almost from the day of independence. The initial pakistani resistence on Bengali as the national language provided the basis for grievances in the East wing against West wing. Later, the grievances took three forms; political, administrative (both civil and military) and economic, as the rulers of Pakistan did not accept the reality that Pakistan was a multilingual and multinational state. They tried to suppress the feelings of Bengali people. Such undemocratic moves were combined with the identity crisis later and gave way to military or authoritarian tendencies in the politics as the political institutions viable to both the units could not develop. Evidences of colonial motivation could be found in Pakistan's fiscal, trade, developmental and even in military policies towards East Pakistan.

Immediately after independence, the gentlemen cadets, who were trained and commissioned from the training academies, who had created a sense of being a part and yet apart from society, started reorganising themselves by reinforcing their professional character and role. Competent oficers got accelerated promotions. A limited number of oficers were sent abroad to U.S., Britain and some commonwealth countries for specialised technical training. Pakistan also started a move to double the training institutions of three services of the armed forces. Even "the battalions and regiments had to be regrouped on the basis of common class composition, common tradition and common recruiting areas." Pakistan purchased arms and ammunition and other military equipment from Britain and from a few other common-wealth countries. So, within short period of time, the Pakistani military became a well organised, well-knit and a modern institution. "Since Pakistan had no ordnance factory, plans were rushed to errect one. By the end of 1951 the first ordance factory was inaugurated at Wah in West Pakistan."[42]

Thus, the major portion of Pakistan's total revenue had been spent to modernise the military apparatus. the Pakistani political leaders. concept of a hostile endiaits India e ts identity crisis a nd its b order tensions w ith afghanistan resulted in boosting the military expenditures. "Pakistan spent 59.51% of total expenditure on defence during the period 1948-59. The rise of defence expenditure during the same period was approximately 116.0%."[43] The budgetary allocations for the military reflected the liberal attitude of political leaders towards armed forces. So, the improved position of military along with deteriorated socio-economic conditions and political instabolity which prevailed after the deaths of Jinnah and Liaquat Ali khan made way for an already politicised military to come actively in politics. So that army of Pakistan could use political power to have lion's share in Pakistan's national cake. But East Pakistan had only 1% of total strength of armed forces in 1947."[44]

41. Hasan Askari Rizvi Op. cit., p. 33.

42. Ibid., p. 34.

43. Calculated from the Table Ibid., pp. 43-44.

44. Ibid., p. 137.

Under the Pakistani recruitment policy also the officer corps who comprised the select elite were carefully screened, they contiuned to come from Punjab and Frontier Province, along with some wealthy immigrants from the United Provinces and Hyderabad with similar class affinities. "Only a handful of Bengali muslims went to the Pakistani army. Punjabi Muslims again constituted at least 60% of the officer corps, with Pathans being the second largest (35%) in independent Pakistan."[45]

Table-2

Military elite in Pakistan, July 1955 (No. of officers)[46]

Service	East Pakistan	West Pakistan
Army	94	894
Navy	7	593
Air Force	60	640

The representation of East Pakistan was exteremely poor in all the three services of the armed forces (See Table : 2). The problem of regional imbalance in the armed forces was partly a legacy of British and partly of West Pakistan's deliberate recruitment policies. "At the time of independece, there was neither a single Bengali regiment nor a cantonment in the eastern half of Bengal because no

45. Anjoos. Upadhyaya; Self Determination in World Politics : Emergence of Bangladesh, (Allahabad : Lokbharti Prakashan, 1984) p. 71.

46. Rounaq Jahan, Pakistan : Failure in National Integration (New York : Columbia University Press, 1972), p. 2

troops were permanently stationed by the British government. In certain wings of army there was not a single Bengali. East Bengal had no military training or pre-cadet training institution. Except during world War-II, no permanent recruiting centres existed there."[47]

Officially, Pakistan government decided to provide for equal opportunity for the people of all languages, but in reality structural dominance of Punjabi thwarted such move. "The Pakistani army raised two battalions of the new East Bengal regiment partly from these pioneers and partly from muslims who had served in the Bihar regiment of the old Indian army."[48] There was however, strong resistance within the dominant Punjabi Pathan military elite to expanding East Pakistan representation in the military. As a result government decided for the policy of gradual induction of Bengalis in the military. A small garrison was stationed in East Pakistan with its newly established headquarters in Dacca to mark the beginning of the Army's presence there. A committee was appointed by Prime Minister Liaquat Ali Khan to inquire into the causes of the paucity of recruits from East Pakistan and to suggest methods to attract recruits from there. By 1958 four exclusive Bengali regiments had been raised. Recruitment to all branches of the military was also opened to East Pakistanis. In 1959 Ayub Khan decieded to reduce physical standards in respect of recruitment of East Pakistanis to the army. These measures helped East Pakistanis to enter

47. Hasan Askari Rizvi, Op. cit. 135.

48. Stephen P. Cohen, Arms and politics in Bangladesh (Buffalow : Council of International Affairs, 1973.). p. 52.

the armed forces but their representation continued to be in very low proportions to their population.

Table-3

East Pakistanis in the armed forces of Pakistan June 1963[49]

Departments	% of East Pakistanis
The Army :	
Junior Commissioned Officers	5
Other ranks	7.8
Officers :	
Army medical corps	23
Navy	19
Technical Officers	9
Chief Petry Officers	21
Leading seamen (around)	28
Air Force	
G.D. Pilot Branch	11
Navigators	31
Administration	27
Education	13
Officers with Foreign Training	
Army	8
JOC	1
Navy	10
Airforce	12

49. Bangladesh Basic Facts Op. cit., p. 31.

Table-4

Propotion of East Pakistanis in the Defence Ministry[50]

Posts	Total	East Pakistan
Class I Officers	29	3
Finance Wing officers	39	1
Directorate General of Civil Aviation	22	1
Deptt. of Ciphers	10	1
Office of the Chief Administrative Officer	59	0
Intersevice Intelligence Directorate	3	0
Aeronautical Inspection	5	1
Airport management Karachi	2	0
Central Engg. Stores	4	3
Civil Aviation Training Unit Karachi, Khore Dacca	3	0
G.C. Military Medical Service	9	1
P.M.A. Kabul	3	0
Army ordance corps	10	2
Inspection and technical Dev. Organ.	8	2
Army stores and clothing, Karachi	10	0
Army inspection depot, Lahore	10	0
Inspector of armaments, Rawalpindi	13	0
Vehicle and engineering equipment chakala	3	0
G.H.Q. Sunde Laboratory	2	0
Formation of Navy	18	1

50. Ibid., p. 32.

The Pakistani civilian as well as military rulers never attempted to broaden the recruitment base of the Pakistani army. Rather, they firmly struck to the myth of martial races created by the British. They used the same argument as used by the British to justify the Punjabi dominated composition of the colonial army, that the Bengalis were short in height and lacked martial tradition. That is why Sayeed says. "although estimates vary, there does not appear to have been more than to 4-6 percent Bengalis in the Pakistani army."[51]

"By 1968 the Bengali share of administrative posts reached a peak of 36%, while 90% of the military manpower continued to be West Pakistani mainly Punjabi and Pathan."[52] This sectional imbalance in the army was not as much inspired by racial and regional traditions as by political considerations. The negligible Bengali representation in Pakistani army added for the political resentment among Bengali personnel.

Inspite of the lack of geographical contiguity the defence planners of Pakistan did not favour a self sustaining defence system for east Pakistan. The keynote to the defence strategy was what Ayub Khan pointed out in 1955, "the defence of the East Pakistan does not lie in that part of the country."[53] He maintained that East Pakistan was not defensible even if the entire military strength was

---

51. Khalid Bin Sayeed, the Political Systems of Pakistan Service of Pakistan (New Haven, 1964) p. 107.

52. Mohammad Ayub, "Pakistan's Political Development, 1947-70 : Birds 'Eyeview' ," Economic and Political Weekly Bombay : Annual Number 1971., p. 69.

53. Quoted in Hasan Askari Rizvi, Op. cit., p. 141.

thrown there as long as the Western base was not made strong.

East Pakistanis demanded the shifting of naval headquarters from Karachi to Chittagong and the setting up of military academies in East Pakistan on the lines of the Kakul and the Risalpur Academies. The demand for the separate military training academies for grounds that the cadet intake from East Pakistan did not justify the duplication of these institutions. Some of the political leaders demanded that every region should be represented in the armed forces in proportion to its population, so as to, "stop recruitment from those areas which are over represented and r ecruit from t hose a reas w hich a re u nder r epresented."[54] After a little relaxation was given in chest Pakistan Air Force by 1965 had risen to about 30% of the total strength.[55]

In 1969 for the first time the GHQ decided that the role of the army was not merely to act as the main source of support and sustainance for a civilian dominated system but to became the main arbiter of the country's destiny. An extremely important factor which contributed to this decision was the state of affairs in East Bengal. The anti-Ayub agitation of the 1968-69 had built up great momentum as a result of the conjunction of the movement for political freedoms in urban West Pakistan and the strong desire for autonomy in East and height measurements, the number of East Pakistanis in the Bengal. In March 1969, President Ayub conceded universal adult fran

54. Ibid., p. 144

55. Mohammad Asghar Khan, Generals in Politics : Pakistan 1958-82 (Delhi : Vikas Publishing House, Ltd. 1983). p. 18.

chise and parliamentay democracy to the opposition leaders, but the situation in East Bengal continued to deteriorate. The concessions were rejected by Sheikh Mujibur Rahman and East Bengal leadership. "The army high command came to the conclusion that active intervention of army both short term and long term in the running of the administration had become essential if the fragile fabric of the Pakistani unity was to be maintained. One may violently disagree with this diagnosis, but the class, professional and regional character of the army made it inevitable that the Government High command reached such a conclusion."[56]

In the Pakistani system it became clear that the greater the threat to the political system and the power structure, the greater was the need for the use of force and for the active participation in routine administration of that final sanction of authority i.e. the armed forces.

Under the military bureaucratic complex in Pakistan, Yahaya Khan assumed power in 1969. The only difference was that while upto 1969, it was the military-bureaucratic element that dominated the complex, the militarism reigned supreme after 1969. After the fall of Ayub regime and the taking over of power by Gen. Yahaya Khan, the military were not at all disposed to giving up their priviledged status in society. The military during this regime became more deeply involved and entrenched in this civilian sphere than before.

The Yahaya Khan martial law regime in the 1969-70 period was a very different from that of the first martial

---

56. N.N. Gidwani, "Genesis and Growth of Pakistan" in S.P. Verma and Virendera Narain (eds). op. cit., p. 26.

law regime under Ayub Khan. "While Yahaya Khan held full powers as Chief Martial Law Administrator (CMLA), he defined his role in very different terms from those that of Ayub had in 1958, as (1) preparations for national elections to a new constituent assembly and (2) encouragement of all political groups, including East Pakistani parties with broad autonomy demands, the Awami league to participate in the political and electoral process."[57] With the announcement of elections to be held by the end of 1970, all the political protest movements of East and West started concentrating on the programmes for elections. During Yahaya regime parallel military officers were attached to civilian officers at all levels of administration hierarchy. "He was a typical representative of the reactionary military-bureaucratic machine. that had by then snuggly fitted into the mantle of their British predecessors."[58]

When Yahaya Khan assumed power, the frustration of East Bengalis had reached its zenith. There were many economic, political and cultural causes for this frustration, but at the end of the dixties, economic reasons appeared to be most important. "If in 1948-49 the per capita income of West Pakistan exceeded that of East Pakistan by 16.7%, in 1960 it was 31.7% and in 1969-70 it became 60 %. East Pakistan earned more than half Pakistan's

57. Leo. E. Rose, "Pakistan : Experiments with Democracy" in Larry Diamond ; Ling and Lipset (eds) Democracy in Asia (New Delhi : Vistaar Publications, 1989) Democracy in Asia (New Delhi : Vistaar Publications, 1989) p. 114.

58. Mohammad Asghar Khan., Op. cit. p21.

export earnings but over 2/3rds of this was earmarked for West Pakistan."[59]

The policy of economic and political discrimination practised by Pakistani ruling elite to the disadvantage of Bengalis, further strengthened the nationalists feelings in East Pakistan. By 1969 nationalism amongst Bengalis had already taken deep roots and with their political suppression, the urge for national consolidation was becoming stronger. "Bengalis now became more aware of the fact that, not only 95% of the budget allocation was going to the benefit of West Pakistan but the entire economic benefit of defence, employment, industries, workshops etc. was also being enjoyed by that region only."[60]

Under these circumstances when nationalist-minded East Bengalis were ensuing elections, the note of Maulana Bhashani's[61] (leader of NAP) speeches emphasised on the need for the establishment of a socialist order which, according to him, was deeply interlinked with the demand for fulfledged provincial autonomy. He also threatened to organise, country wide strikes, peasants rallies and ultimately guerrilla warfare with a 30,000 strong army, if his demands were not conceded. Sheikh Mujibur Rahman, in his election campaign concentrated on the six point formula of the Awami league and the eleven point charter of the East Bengal students which emphasised both

---

59. Joseph Stern, "Growth, Development and Regional Equity in Pakista", In Falcon and Papanek (ed.) Development Policy : The Pakistan Experience, (Harvard University Press, 1971). p. 39.

60. Anjoo S. Upadhyaya, Op. pp. 79-80

61. S.K. Chakravarti, Op. cit. p. 179.

pronvincial autonomy and the establishment of a socialist order.[62]

President Yahaya Khan postponed the elections to be held in October 5, 1970 till December 7, 1970. Sheikh Mujibur Rahman reacted as, "They (i.e. the rulers of Pakistan) have had enough of the crimes in the name of 'national integration... Bangladesh is now awaken...If the polls are frustrated, the people of the Bangladesh will owe it to the million, who have died to make the supreme sacrifices and sacrifices another million lives, if need be, so that was can live as a free people and so that Bangladesh can be master of its own destiny."[63] Further added, "if the people of Bengal failed to wrest their usurped rights, they would continue to live like slaves in their own soil which had so long been treated as virtual colony."[64] He expressed, "Grave and challenging problems including those of hunger, unemployment, illiteracy and floods among others lie ahead, we, pledge to do every thing possible with the active support and cooperation of the people, so that we may look forward to a better future."[65]

The December, 1970 elections were held on schedule. The election results were unexpected both in the eastern and western wings. The Awami league own all but two of the seats allocated to East Pakistan in the constituent assembly. Thus, gaining an absolute majority for the party, despite the fact that it had not contested a single seat in

62. Ibid.
63. Quoted in S.K. Chakravarty, Op. cit., pp. 181.82.

64. The People Dacca, Oct. 21.1970.
65.The Dawn, Karachi, Dec 20, 1970.

the western wing, the new Pakistan People's Party (ppp), founded by zulfikar bhutto, won a majority of the seats.

Yahaya Khan as backed by Bhutto and other western politicians used military force in Bengal but, the present propular mood was all for complete independence.

The poor representation of East Pakistan in the military was added to the list of grievences against the central government when the agitation for autonomy was launched by Awami League. The military was viewed as a symbol of West Pakistani or Punjabi domination, which widened the gap between East and West Pakistan. When Yahaya Khan refused to tranfer power after 1970 elections, Bengalis described the military as the main obstacle in the way of implementation of electoral verdict. The military and the Bengalis. This reinforced their conviction that the military rulers were treating them like l colonised people. The level of violence in East Pakistan became acute in personal crimes, attacks on supporters of Ayub regime, in Bihari-Bengali conflicts and in communal disorders. The East Pakistan Police became increasingly alienated from the West Pakistan troops in the province and there was trouble between them. Awami league leaders developed the notion of massive army attack. Guerilla forces also supported Bangladesh forces, these factors gave rise to civil-war. "All the professionally trained men from East Pakistan rifles, East Bengal regiment and Bengali police deserted and joined the ranks of Awami league and formed the main core of Mukti Bahini which operated as a guerilla force."[66]

---

66. Hasan Askari Rizvi, Op. cit. 187.

The atrocities of Pakistani army went on increasing and reached its peak. "Since the last week of March, 1971 refugees began pouring into India. The number of refugees as on September 9, 1971 was 8, 428,745. India spent on an average 28 million rupees a day on refugges,"[67] which was a great burden on her economy. The financial burden of refugee relief was estimated by the world Bank, at about $ 700 million in a full year. This was nearly half of India's defence budget in 1970, and the nation groaned under the additional economic pressure.[68]

Prime minster Indira Gandhi in the broadcast to the nation on dec. 3' 1971 said'

since last march' we have born the heaviest burden and withstood the greatest pressure, in a tremendous effort to urge the world to help in bringing about a peaceful solution and preventing the annihilation of an entire people, whose only crime was to vote for democracy. But the world ignored the basic causes and concerned itself only with certain repercussions. The situation was bound to deteriorate and the courageous bound to deteriorate and the courageous band of freedom fighters have been staking their all in defence of the values for which we also have struggled, and which are basic to our way of life.

Today that war in Bangladesh has become a war on India. This has imposed upon me, my people and the gov

---

67. "Influx of Refugees from Bangladesh : Analysis," International Conference on Bangaldesh held from Sep, 18 to Oct. 20, 1971 in I.D.S.A., N. Delhi (Document XIX), p. 1.

68. Effect of Refugee Inflow on Economy, World Bank Report, in Asian Recorder, Vol. XVII, No. 41, p. 10400.

ernment of India, a great responsibility. We have no other option but to put our country on a war footing. Our brave officers and jawans are at their post mobilised for the defence of the country. An emergency has been declared for the whole of India. Every necessary step is being taken, and we are prepared for all eventualities...We are peace loving people, but we know that peace can not last if we do not guard our democracy and our way of life. so today, we fight not merely for territorial integrity, but for the basic ideals which have given strength to this country and on which alone, we can progress to a better future...Aggression must be met, and the people of India will meet it with fortitute and determination and with discipline and utmost unity."[69]

On the other hand, Yahaya Khan in his broadcast to the nation on Dec. 4, 1971 said,

"We are at war with a cunning and cruel enemy. We will defend our country at any price and at every sacrifice. We are confident that in this war for the integrity of our country, we will have the sympathy and help of all our friends and nations, who are on the side of justice and peace. They will undoubtedly severly condemn Indian aggression and support our right to defent the country."[70]

The war, thus broke out between India and Pakistan. India liberated Bangladesh with the help of Mukti Bahini, an armed wing of Awami league.

---

69. Bangladesh Documents, Vol. II (New Delhi : Government Printing Press, 1971), p. 183.

70. Ibid, p. 185.

Pakistan and India deployed forces against each other on various fronts[71]:-

Tabe-5

Fronts	India	Pakistan
East	7 infantry division	6 infantry division
	400 combat air craft	20 combat air craft
China	6 infantry division	----------
West	1 tank division	2 tank divisions
	12 infantry divisioin	11 infantry divisions
	100 combat aircrafts	360 combat aircrafts

Notes : (1) India's main tank divisions remained uncommitted during the struggle.

(2) India's independent bridges were in the East.

(3) Pakistan's military bridges were in the West.

"The crackdown took a terrible toll : perhaps 1000,000 dead, 10 million refugees and untold thousands homeless, hungry and sick."[72] The Bangladesh independence movent which essentially belonged to the category of nationalist revolutionary guerrilla operations characteristically began as an uprising against the reign of terror, therefore, it bagan first and organised later. Sheikh Mujibur Rahman had not organised it at the grassroot level. Rather, he had not organised it at the grassroot level. Rather,

71. Sisir Gupta, "Why India Won the Fourteen Day War," Armed forces Journal April, 1972. p. 48.

72. Time Magazine, (U.S.A.), Dec. 20, 1071, p. 28.

he had spurned suggestion of certain Bengali officers of Pakistan's armed forces who had contacted him to organise the movement on the lines of armed forces action. The independence war had been successfully protracted at the strategic level for eight months until the time the Indian Army was in a fit position to intervene physically in East Pakistan. The guerrilla leaders had secured total support from the local people for the movement against Pakistani government. Guerrillas succeeded in wearing down the militarily superior Pakistani forces. A direct action against enemy forces was evident. "Sabotage and terrorism had multiplied manifold : collaborators and known reactionary elements w ere a ssiduously sought and liquidated. People's courts were administering justice. vulnerable military and polic outposts were being sujected to continued guerrilla attack and weak enemy columns were repeatedly ambushed. This yielded substantial quantity of arms, equipment, medical supplies and radio equipment is in amply evident by exploits of the Mukti Bahini, The whole nation had been motivated to achive liberation and it had asserted itself to the optimum extent.[73] The Mukti Bahini continued to expand its freedon struggle. "The first batch of 700 trained guerrillas soon swelled in 10,000 guerrilla consisting of 30,000 regular and 70,000 irregular guerrillas Gram Parishads villages of East Bengal had formed rural guerrilla sancturies which facilitated the expansion of the movement. Similarly the organisation of the Sangram Samitis (Revolutionary Council) helped the ex-

73. Capt. S.K. Garg (Retd.) Spotlight : Freedom Fighters of Bangladesh (New Delhi : Allied publishers Pvt. Ltd., 1984) p. 181.

pansion of the freedom struggle."[74]

The Bengali armed forces in East-Pakistan at that time (1971) were six battalians of the East Bengal Regiment (E.B.R.) numbering about 6000 men, plus, 14000 tightly armed troops of the border security force, the East Pakistan Rifles (E.P.R.). In addition, there were some 45,000 police in the province.[75]

Gen. Osmany, retired East Pakistani army officer who took command of the Bangladesh liberation forces during the war, later came to say that, "Bengali personnel in the army might well have stayed neutral, had the Pakistani atrocities confined their crackdown to selected Bengali politicians. It was the overkill, the sўstematic 'elitocide' campaign to exterminate professionals, intellectuals and army officers that decided them to revolt."[76] Such armed forces later played active role in the politics of Bangladesh.

The liberation war of 1971, put the finishing touch on the politicisation of armed forces of Bangladesh and radicalised a section of the freedom fighters so much that they became revolutionary in their ideas. The young freedom fighters became conscious of political power and experienced the need of change of the power in their own favour if their objectives are not met with. So, the liberation war brought closer or even merged civilian and mili

74. Ibid, p. 183.

75. Maj. Gen. D.K. Palit The Lightning Campaign : The Indo-Pakistan War. 1971 (Salisbury : Compton Press, 1972) p. 54.

76. Quoted in Alan Lindquist, "Military and Development in Bangladesh ," IDSA. Bulletin (Institution of Development in studies). Vol. IX, No.1, July, 1977, p. 11.

tary personnel, which made military personnel to understand the fragile fabric of political institutions. Thus, Bangladesh came into existence through various traumatic experiences inheriting a highly politicised army.

IV-Military and Political Institutions

Military derives the opportunity to play its role in politics, not only from the prevailing socio-economic conditions but also from the level of political institutonalisation and the structure of the society. In particular, they lie in the absence or weakness of effective political institutions in the society."[1] Huntington refers to such societies as 'praetorian' societies, in which all main groupings in society are both politicised and given a direct action. It follows that military is also politicised and given a direct action in these societies.

The Bangladesh society can be termed as a 'praetorian society as there is high social mobilisation and low level of intitutionalisation. The society also has low level of political culture. Political culture is not necessarily static, as it may change very quickly.

"The notion of political culture assumes that the attitudes, sentiments and congnitions that form and govern political behaviour in any society are not just random con geries but represent coherent patterns which fit together and are mutually reinforcing. In spite of the great potenti-

---

1. Samuel p. Huntington, Political Order in Changing Societies, (New Haven : Yale University Press, 1968), p. 194.

alities for diversity in political orientations, in any particular community, there is a limited and distinct political culture, which gives meaning to the polity, discipline to institutions and social relevance to individual acts."[2]

The "praetorianism" deals with the rate of mobilisation vis-a-vis institutionalisation where as the culture is a set pattern of norms. Bangladesh is definitely a "preastorian state." The proper functioning of the government needs institutions with high degree of differentiation and specialisation. Failure of the development of such institutions results in the failure of political systems paving the way for military interventions. The social change and rapid mobilisation places an enormous burden on political institutions. In the process of social change the growth in secularisation, economic and commercial development, urbanisation improve the position of some social classes and deteriorate that of others, new groups enter the political arena, new kinds of allengiances develop and increased demands on government arise, all of which strain the political framework and weaken the political institutions. Therefore, complexity adaptablity and autonomy are necessary for viability of political institutions.

According to Almond and Powell[3] a society faces four problems-state building, nation building, participation and distribution. Political modernisation conflict with

---

2. Lucian W. Pye, "Political Culture and Political Development" in Lucian Pye and Sidney Verba (ed), Political Culture and Political Development, (New Jersy : Princeton, 1965), p. 7.

3. G. Almond and G. Bingham Powell jr, Comparative Politics : A Developmental Approach (New Delhi : Amerind Publications Pvt. Ltd. 1972), p. 35.

parochialism and integrated centralised institution is welcome for state building. This results in the formation of penetrative bureaucracy to cope with the situation.

Nation-building deals with the cultural aspect. But, there are many cases in which centralised and penetrative bureaucracies have been created, while a homogenous pattern of loyality and commitment to the central political institutions has never emerged, as in the case of Bangladesh. Rapid increase in volume and intensity of participation i.e. that demands for a share in the decision-making process of a political system weakens the political system. The failure of affective distribution also results in the failure of system. Thus participation crises and penetration crises threaten identity and legitimacy of democratic system. So, it is the capacity of the system to develop effective institutions which answers its stability. In the absence of this capability, the degree of bureaucratisation, centralisation and militarisation increases. therefore, for a stable political system there is need for the specialised political infrastructure, the development of sub-systems such as political parties, pressure groups, bureaucracy, legal system, concensual constitution and the media of mass communication.

"In the democratic systems this political infrastructure consists of relatively autonomous institutions, while in totalitarian systems the media of mass communication, interest groups of various kinds and political parties are all closely, hierarchically articulated with the ruling elite and bureaucracy. They are subordinated to the government rather than being relatively independent of it and able to transmit impulses, demands and proposals from the society."[4]

"Political party, an organised institution, r elating elites and masses in terms of political goals and concentrating at least manifestly on recruitment to elite offices, is less than two centuries old, whereas military and bureaucratic organisations have ancient historical roots."5

The longevity of institution in comparative term has credited the military to be more effective and disciplined organisation.

The political elites in the underdeveloped areas rely upon political change, particularly to provide new standards of legitimacy and orderly patterns of mobilised political participation. The party system defines the nature of constitutional future of polity and nature of society. However, the effectiveness with which political parties carry on socialisation activities depends upon the internal characteristics of the party as well as on conditions of political and social environment.

Along with the political parties and pressure groups the governmental institutions for rule making, rule application and rule adjudications should be effective to cope with the emerging challenges from the system. For rule making where should be effective legislatives. Bureaucracies are charged with rule application. Bureaucracies are of enormous importance in the performance of political system as they are multifuncitonal. But to keep the bureaucracy on the rails there should be an effective ruling and derective group. Without such a group bureaucracy may get involved in a range of political functions and provide for a military or a civil clique as the ruling element in

4. Ibid, p. 47.
5. Ibid, p. 115.

the political system, as in Bangladesh. The rule adjudication needs an independent judiciary to perform its function autonomously and impartially. So, the ineffective development of various instituions in the political systems leads to its decay. Like many other developing countries, Bangladesh also could not develop differentiated, adoptive, autonomous and cumulative governmental structures.

Thus, the democracies survice only if they provide effective government. Breakdown in the continuity of democracy comes about when consensus breaks,

"When some powerful minority within a population revolts in response to what it believed to be a gross failure under one or more of the three basic categories of national policy : policy towards national security, domestic welfare, or the provision of justice under existing constitutional arrangements. Such ruptures have been brought about by a volatile organised minority, when the majority was probably against the active minority or simply apathetic, disorganised or uncertain."[6]

Like all other nations of developing world Bangladesh wanted quick polotical developments emphasising upon governemtal performance and a greater capacity for carrying out public policies. This process of development resulted in the development of the institution of bureaucracy. The bureaucracy was developed and compared to legislature because of colonial legacy of Pakistan and Britishers. But bureaucracy was extractive and regulative in nature than goal orinted. Bureaaucracies, thus, came up as institutions for interest articulation of various inter-

---

6. W.W. Rustow, Politics and the Stages of Growth (London : Cambridge Universty Press, 1971), p. 271.

ests groups whereas in democratic polity this function is assigned to political party.

After gaining independence the Bangladesh constituent assembly passed the constitution for the Peopls's Republic of Bangladesh on November 5, 1972, this constitution came into effect on December 16, 1972. With the adoption of constitution the state became constitutionally wedded to the principles of nationalism, democracy, socialism and secularism. "The constitution's attempt to synthesise democracy with socialism was popularly known as Mujibism."[7]

Like Indian Constituion, Bangladesh provided for fundamental rights. Excepting the right to property, all other human rights were listed. The rule of law, fundamental human rights, freedom, euqality and justice-political, economic and social had been guaranteed for the citizens.

In order to establish a just and egalitarian society, the constitution provided for socialist economic system. To end communalism in Bangladesh, the constitution makers emphasised on the principle of secularism in constitution. Communalism was outlawed and religious bigotry had been made strictly punishable. These principles were combined on the basis of Bengali identity.

The constitution provided for unitary form of government in parliamentary democracy with the executive powers of the republic exercisable by the Prime Minister. The cabinet was responsible to the parliament. All execu tive actions of the government were to be taken in the name of the President of the State.

---

7. Abul Fazal Huq, "Constitution Making in Bangladesh." Pacific Affairs, Vol. XLVI, No. 1, Spring, 1973, p. 72.

The constitution provided for the unicameral legislature consisting of 300 members out of whom 285 had to be directly elected on the basis of adult franchise and the remaining fifteen had be chosen by the parliament from among the women of the country. With enormous powers, the parliament of the country was, thus, supreme under the constitution of 1972. It was called 'Jatiya Sangsad.'[8]

All matters relating to formation and deployment of the armed forces of the country were placed under the control of parliament. Under the events of emergency arising out of war, the parliament could suspent, some provisions of the constitution. President had the powers to interfere and to take necessary actions under such situations. But under such situations parliament had to be summoned immediately in order to enact the emergency laws. The President was supreme commander of armed forces, but in exercising this command he was to abide by the decisions of the parliament. President was thus a titular head of the state.

Constitution[9] also provided for decentralisation in administration and planning, implementation of public order by elected local bodies, provided for reorganisation of civil bureaucracy including the power to change the conditions of service and measures against the members of parliament of party defection. It provided for an inde pendent judiciary with further provisions for the high court

---

8. Ibid., p. 73.

9. See Government of People's Republic of Bangladesh, Ministry of Law and Parliamentary Affairs, The Constitution of People,s Republic of Bangladesh (Dhaka : December, 1972), Part I & II.

division of the supreme court to hold sessions at places other than its permanent seat in the capital. The constitution initiated a democratic life of political institution in Bangladesh and drew people in a powerful democratic movement to reshape their destiny in future.

The constitution was framed by a Constituent Assembly formed by the constituent assembly of Bangladesh order 1972, under the proclamation of Independence of 10 April, 1971, It consisted of all East Pakistan members elected to the National Assembly of Pakistan and the Provincial Assembly of East Pakistan in the first General elections held between December, 1970 and March, 1971. Signed by 357 members and authenticated by the speaker of the constitution became effective from December 16, 1972. The constitution was framed by the constituent assembly was represented by the ruling Awami League. It was framed under the influence of Mujib.[10] Many political faction, at the dawn of independence, were banned. Military and other interest groups were not taken into consideration. Later, therefore, military takeovers altered the basic nature of constitution. Lack of representation of various groups and political factions in the constituent assembly later proved disastrous, inhibiting the proper funcitioning of the constitution.

After the enactment of the constitution, the Awami League governement held the first General Elections in liberated Bangladesh on March 7, 1973. The Awami League secured 292 out of 300 seats.[11] The elections did not

10. Abul Fazal Huq, Op. cit, p. 74.

11. Bangladesh Observer, (Dhaka) March 11, 1973.

bring any major change either in the executive or in the legislature.

Sheikh Mujibur Rehman became Prime Minister and Justice Abu Sayeed Chowdhury was elected President by the Parliament. Under the leadership of Awami League, its basic attitude of not allowing the legislature the power to scrutinise the executive did not change. Parliament, thus, could play only a limited role. The Cabinet headed by Sheikh Mujib, thus, enjoyed absolutes and unaccountable legislative and executive authority. "Paliament met only for 118 days during its two and half years life from March 1972 to 1975. During this period it enacted about 140 legislations. But 85 of these had been promulgated as ordinances by the president and placed before parliament for re-enacting as laws."[12]

The ordinance making power intended to meet urgent situations. But the government used this power indiscriminately to deal with ordinary or normal matters like, the fixation of remuneration and privileges of ministers. Most of the amendment bills were brought by the opposition M.P.'s. But not a single amendment moved by them was accepted by the government. Though some of the opposition's amendment motions were of the same effect as those of the treasury benches, that were accepted by the house. Besides, the bills were passed in such a hurry that the M.P.'s could not get ample time for discussion. Moinuddin Ahmed, an opposition M.P., observed, "the bills are coming and passing (the House) like fast running trains

---

12. U.A.B. Raiza Akhtar Banu, "The Fall of Sheikh Mujibur Rehman : An Analysis", 'Indian Political Science Review', Vol. XV, No. 1, Jan, 1981, p.7.

in such a way that many of the members of the House are incapable of catching them."

The ruling Awami League party was coalition of various factions which had come together for the purpose of liberation of Bangladesh. Although, Awami League supported the four pillars of Mujibism : democracy, nationalism, socialism and secularism, various factions of Awami League started giving more attention to their personal interests, which later on, resulted in rivalaries and factionalism within the ruling party.

After independence when Awami league (AL) formed government in Bangladesh, it faced virtually no political opposition. The right wing parties like Jamaat-i-Islam (JI), all the factions of Muslim League (ML), the Nizam-i-Islam, the Jamaat-ul-Ulema-i-Islam (JUI) and the Pakistan Democratic party (PDP) which had collaborated with Pakistani army during the liberation war were all banned. The left wing parties were allowed to function. However, "opposition to Awami League regime developed very quickly. There was opposition from the far left and the far right, which the regime branded as 'Naxalites' and 'Razakars'."[14]

In order to crush such forces Mujib gave rise to his own army 'Rakhi Bahini' thus regular army was annoyed because of further politicization of army on the basis of

---

13. Abul Fazal Huq, "The Parliament and Politics of Bangladesh (1973-82), South Asian Studies, Vol. XXII, No. 2, July-Dec, 1987, p.27

14. A. W. Bhuiyan, "Bangladesh Politics : Continuity Amidst Change", Indian Political Science Review, Vol. XVI, No. 1, Jan. 1982, p. 23.

ideology. Dissidence within Awami League was initially a major source of opposition in Bangladesh, After independence some members of the Awami League students wing, the Students League (SL) led by ASM abdur Rab and Shahjahan Siraj began to criticise AL's policy and formed a separate group.[15] Another group of students leagues (SL) was led by Nur-e-Alam Siddiqui. This split was follwoed by split in A.L. labour front as well as in A.L. affiliated Mukti Juddha Sangsad. Association of freedom fighters was named as the Jatio Mukti Juddha Sangram Parishad. Finally on October 31, 1972, a new party called Jatio Samajtantrik Dal (JSD) was formed with ASM. Abdur Rab and Maj. M.A. Jalil as joint convenors. JSD weas opposed to the nationalist leadership of A.L. it supported Bangladesh Communist League (BCL), an underground party led by Serajul Alam Khan. National Awami Party (Bhashani) in the beginning supported Mujib but later on supported S arbohar's party, posing a se rious threat to Mujib. Some Communist parties which emerged were Purba Banglar Communist Party, Banglar Communist Party, East Pakistani Communist Party, the Sarbohar Party etc.

Mujib's Awami League was itself faction ridden. All the parties were organisationally very weak, they revolved around the personality of their leaders. Ideological differences amongst these parties were nominal. Opposition was unorganised. All such weaknesses in the political parties paved an easy way for the armed forces to paly a political role.

Like political parties the pressure groups were not

15. See The Holiday (Dacca), July 27, 1972.

well organised. All the parties had their students and peasants wings but all of them were again faction-ridden without any strong organisation.

In the newly independent Bangaladesh the socio-political environment was not favourable, for the dominant position and elitism of the bureaucrats as, they were not held in high esteeem in Bangladesh because of their association with the military rulers during the last twelve years. "The 1972 constitution of Bangladesh denied the king of constitutional especially in Pakistan, under the 1956 and 1962 constitution. Article 134 of 1972 Constitution stipulated that, civil servants shall hold office during the pleasure of the president and the article 135 (3) stated that the 'decision thereon of the authority empowered to dismiss or remove such person or to reduce him rank shall be final."[16]

After introducing the parliamentary form government, the planning commission wrote, "They (bureaucrats) can be neither i nnovator, nor catalytic agents for a social change. It is only a political cadre with firm roots in the people and motivated by the new ideology and willing to live and work among the people as one of them can mobilise the masses and transform their pattern of behaviour."[17] The Prime Minister, Sheikh Mujibur Rahman argued, that, "the colonial rulers had built up the bureaucracy as a sepa-

---

16. The Constitution of People's Republic of Bangladesh, (Dhaka : Constituent Assembly, 1972), pp. 54-55

17. The First Five Year Plan 1973-78, Planning Commission, (Dhaka : Government of People,s Republic of Bangladesh, 1972), p. 4.

rate class with special safeguards in their own interests." He further emphasized, "We do not want to keep this class-Bureaucrats must change their mentality. They must realise that they are not rulers they are servants."[18]

In the independent Bangladesh the bureaucracy like all other political organisations became seriously affected by sachism and factionalism. A large number of the senior posts in the Secretariat were occupied by civil-servants who had belonged to the former East Pakistan Civil-Service. Moreover, many important administrative positions were held by persons who in liberation struggle and were rewarded with such appointments. Many business executives were also appointed to manage industrial and financial agencies, that were nationalised during 1972-73. The bureaucracy during early years of independence remained dissatisfied. Most of the important positions were taken over by the political men. Bureaucracy became opportunistic and there was tremendous in rise politicals sycophancy. Bureaucratic institution got totally degenerated.

Later, in the ruling Awami League, The intra-party conflicts became more pronounced. The socio-economic conditions deteriorated. To face the various problems government started increasing repression, especially through the armed band, Rakhi Bahini. Most of the repressive measures were against the radical left. "Although initially Mujib managed to balance the various forces within Bangladesh society, the basic contradictions within the nationalist movement could not be resolved. As a dominant class the petty bourgeoise leadership of the Awami League became

18. Quoted in M. Nazrul Islam, "Crisis of Politics in Bangladesh," South Asian Studies, Vol. XXIV, No. 2, July-dec, 1987, p.89.

pre-occupied with keeping the revolutionary potential of the people within narrow limits in order to remain in power. Although its ideological rhetoric remained leftist, its politics turned increasingly to wards right."[19]

The Awami League now incorporating all the progressive political parties and professional groups rechristened as Bangladesh Krishak Shramik Awami League (BAKSAL) could be more effective in dealing with anti-national forces. The government, thus, seized one-party power through the Fourth Amendment in January, 1975. All opposition parties were banned. The members of parliament were allowed either to join BAKSAL or quit. One party presidential rule was established in the country under the leadership of Mujib. It was provided that Mujib, the father of the nation would be the President of the country for a period of five years from the date of constitutional amendment. Mujib was accused of being a dictator. Soon after taking oath as the new president, Mujib described the constitutional change as his "second revolution"[20] to wipe out the anti-state elements, terrorists, hoarders and smugglers and to bring about the democracy to the exploited masses.

The main features of fourth amendment were :[21]

(a) President to be directly elected for five years and the president incumbent was to resign in favour of the in

---

19. Kirsten Westergaard, State and Rural Society in Bangladesh, (Curzon Press, Scandavian Institute of Asian Studies, Monograph series no. 49, 1985) p. 80.

20. Bangladesh Observer, Dhaka, Jan. 26, 1975.

21. Syamali Ghosh, "Constitutional Changes in Bangladesh : Process and Political Development," India Quarterly, Vol. XIII, No. 4, Oct-Dec., 1986. p. 396.

cumbent Prime-minister as if he had been so elected.

(b) President was removable by three fourth votes of the Parliament for violating the Constitution, grave misconduct, physical or mental disability.

(c) The existing Parliament was to continue for another five years unless dissolved by the President.

(d) President was to appoint a Vice-president and a Prime-Minister and Council of Ministers to aid and advise him.

(e) President might establish a single national political party automatically dissolving all other political parties and would chalk out the details of such a party.

(f) Members of parliament refusing to join such a party or ignoring its instructions were to loose their seats.

(g) Special courts, tribunals or commissions to be appointed by the parliament to enforce the fundamental rights.

(h) President could remove judges on grounds of misbehaviour or incapacity.

(i) The system of local governments by elected representatives was abolished.

The parliament, however, retained its power to amend the constitution as per the provisions of the 1972 constitution. But the features of fourth amendment led to the democratic polity of Bangladesh towards an authoritarian one. Democratic process was thus nipped in the bud.

This constitutional change in Bangladesh marked a wide departure from the conventional liberal democratic framework. The introduction of one party state was perhaps the most important factor that alienated the Awami

League from political forces and provided justification for the military intervention of 15th August, 1975.

When Mujib lost faith in the organisation of Awami League, he started relying more and more on the bureaucracy. The administrative elites, thus, began to recover their position. The increasing active participation of these elites in the affairs of the state and their adroit performance, especially in the maintenance of law and order and raising the productivity of law and order and raising the productivity in the nationalised sector brought them in the forefront and them these elites in alliance with the military officers started managing the affairs of the state. Bureaucracy, thus, became one of the most important decision-making institution in the country.

The democratic political institutions under Mujib regime could not develop as, Mujib led the politics of the country towards authoritarianism. The political institutions developed by Mujib were not able to meet the rising demands of the people. On august 15, 1975 Mujib was assassinated in a plot led by a group of Majors in the Bangladesh army. His system collapsed with his death. The young coup makers installed khondakar Mushtaq Ahmed as president, who was foreign trade minister in the Mujib Cabinet but was known for his anti-Mujib feelings. The coup was the result of personal vengeance of young military officers. They just wanted to liquidate the Sheikh dynasty. They did not have any policy perspectives or any leadership syndicate. After attaining presidency, Khondakar Musktaq Ahmed promised elections and return to parliamentary government. But after a series of coups and counter coups Maj. Gen. Zia-ur-Rahman Chief Martial Law Administrator (C.M.L.A) emerged as the defacto ruler of the country. He was neither bound by the 1972 constitution nor by the IVth amendment. But the provisions of IV amendment were retained by him to consolidate his power. On April 21, 1977, he assumed presidency. He was confirmed in presidency in May, 1977 when a referendum was held. The electorate were asked to endorse the 19-point programme of socio-economic development and reform (See Appendix-II). "Zia obtained unprecedented 88.5 percent turnout of votes and 98.88 percent affirmative votes. The results, however, seemed to be the out come of unfair means in the referendum."[22] In June, 1978 he was elected president for a five year term in election. Zia won a landslide victory by securing 76-67 percent of the 53-59 percent voter turnout.[23]

"The constitution as it stood under Zia called for a President elected by a plurality popular vote and a single chamber parliament (Jatiyo Sangsad) elected, also by plurality vote from 300 single member constituencies. In addition the parliament itself was to elect by proportional vote a number of women members. The President appointed Prime Minister vote from 300 single member constituencies. In addition the parliament itself was to elect by proportional vote a number of women members. The President appointed Prime Minister from among the members of the parliament who had the support of majority. The President also appointed other members of the cabinet. He could not select more than 1/5th of the cabi

---

22. Veena Kukreja ; Civil-Miltary Relations in South Asia : Pakistan, Bangladesh and India, (Delhi : Sage Publications, 1991), p. 168.

23. Ibid.

net members from outside the parliament. President had the powers to dismiss the cabinet. All the laws were passed by the president. Power was thus centered in the office of the President."[24] (See Chart-I)

Chart-I

President
(Directly Elected for a five years term)

Vice-President
(Appointed by president)

Parliament
(300 directly elected seats, additional women candidated elected by Parliament, voting by proportional vote, all five years term)

Prime Minister
(Appointed by the President, must have the condifence of Parliament)

Cabinet
(Varying number, political heads of ministries and depart ments, upto 1/5th may be from out side parliament)

Civil Service

---

24. Craig Baxter and Yogender Malik, Charles H. Kenney and Robert C. Obert, Government and Politics in South Asia, (London : westview Press, 1987), pp. 159-61.

The government at the centre was organised into a number of departments of ministries. The active head of the department or ministry was a secretary drawn from civil service. Although an increase had occured in the number of persons from the police service and occasionally, the military personal served in secretarial positions.

Judiciary, the watchdog of democracy which remained under the influence of authoritarian leadership of Mujib since the independence of Bangladesh, lost its significance under the military rule of Zia.

The supreme court of bangladesh had two divisions. The Appellate Division, as its name indicates had only appellate jurisdiction. The high court division had both appellate jurisdiction and some original jurisdiction. The Supreme Court had benches in several cities besides Dhaka. However, there were district courts and up Zilla Courts also.[25] The judges were recruited by the President, as was provided in the IVth amendment. Thus judiciary was not separated from the executive. Executive dominated over judiciary as well. There is no court verdict so far in history of Bangladesh jurispudence, which curtailed the state power. Thus governmental and political institutions were undifferentiated, cenralised and subordinate to the whims of the ruler. The whole performance in these institutions became paternalised.

President was not bound by the 1972 constitution, instead he brought many constitutional changes in order to consolidate and legitimise his rule stating that, "there is much resentment among people against some of the

---

25. Ibid.

fundamental principles and provisions of the constitution. Hence necessary constitutional amendments are being promulgated to reflect the attitude and hopes and aspirations of the people of the country."[26] He tried to consolidate his power through local government institutions composed of re-presentatives of areas concerned. The amendments provided for the identity of the people of Bangladesh. The citizens of Bangladesh who were known as Bangalees under the constitution were now to be known as Bangladeshis and Islam replaced secularism in the constitution of Bangladesh. By all mesasures Zia tried to establish the rule of an all powerful president under a demo-cratic facade. He decreed several amendments to the constitution, which he later managed to ratify by the parliament. For, the parliament itself had been elected under terms and conditions set by the president and not by the constitution and could be summoned, prorogued or dissolved by him at his will.

Zia reduced parliamentary institution to a rubber stamp and the whole system under him in reality, was authoritarian. All the political institutions were made to suit the wishes of all powerful President. Zia aimed at new authoritarianism through a pseduo-democratic process with a grassroot party network for recruitment of support groups at the village level.

In his civilianisation process he introduced 19-point programme for the economic upliftment of the masses. Zia carried on political negotiations and realignments with political parties. Thus, zia slowly started turning from a

---

26. See Bangladesh Observer, 23 April, 1977.

'soldier' to a 'politician'. (See Appendix-II). In fact, 19-point programme was a blue print of advancement and planning in order to legitimize his rule.

He also announced for holding general elections in the country expressing full faith in restoring democracy. He said,

"I and my government believe in full democracy and are determined to restore government of the elected representatives of the people in due time. The people are the source of all powers and it is our goal to reflect fully the hopes and aspirations of people in every action and policy of the government. The government has decided to take certain steps to this end."[27] (See Appendix-i)

His regime was composed of at least three different streams of political forces[28] : (i) His own factional supporters within the army and bureaucracy. (ii) Right-wing muslim league, and other Islamic fundamentalists who were either eliminated or suppressed by Sheikh Mujib because of his secular politics and (iii) A major chunk of radical force who were opposed to Sheikh Mujib. Thus, it is clear that almost all factions which were against Shiekh Mujib were included in his civil-military coalition.

The changes made in the constitution either by Mujib or Zia for consolidation of power indicate that there was no consensus even on preamble of the Constitution. Thus, identity crises and legitimacy crises paved the way for military intervention and retention of military in the poli-

---

27. See Appendix-I, For full text of rhe President's address to the nation.

28. See Keesing's Contemporary Archives, Oct. 15, 1976, p. 27989.

tics of Bangladesh.

Zia's Vice-president Justice Abdus Sattar formed a new party named Jatiyatabadi Ganotantrik Dal (known as JAGODAL).[29] The party was formed to see the response of political forces and elements within the country. The party was not joined by Zia. JAGODAL, however failed to recruit 'political heavy-weights'. Zia contested elections in 1978 as a nominee of the JAGODAL along with five other small parties who had electoral alliance, jatiyabadi Front (J.F.). In his campaign Zia emphasized, on "bangladeshi Nationalism instead of foreignism; people's democracy in place of palace politics and economic self reliance instead of dependence on foreign powers."[30]

The President said "We should be inspired by the great ideas of modesty, self-restraint tolerance and patriotism," and urged all to accept the elections in a democratic manner. "Let us move forward to the path of tolerance, perseverence and peace in the interest of the people and the country, forgetting hatred, quarrels and difference."[31] The opposition political parties accused Zia of being a military dictator.[32] The opposition parties joined together in a common platform called Ganotantrik Oikyo Jote (Democratic United Front) with retired Gen. M.A.G.

---

29. M. Rashiduzzaman, "Bangladesh in 1978 : Search for a Political Party," 'Asian Survey, Vol. XIX, No. 2, 1979, p. 235.

30. Rounaq Jahan, quoted in M.Q. Zaman, "Ziau Rahman Leadership Styles and Mobilization Policies," Indian Political Science Review, Vol XVIII, No. 2, July 1984, p. 199.

31. See Appendix-III, For full text of Zia,s address to the nation.

32. Keesings Contemporary Archives, 15 Sep. 1978, p. 29197.

Osmani.[33] Zia won the elections by unfree and unfair means.[34]

After complete concentration of power in his hands, Zia launched his own party-'Bangladesh Nationalist Party' which replaced JAGODAL. "B.N.P. was remarkably similar to the A.L. and indeed P.M.L. (Pakistan Muslim League) of the Ayub Khan-Monem Khan era. For that matter it was the grand daughter of the old Muslim League. Often, even the people were the same."[35] In the Parliamentary elections held in January, 1979, the B.N.P. won 207 out of 300 general seats of Parliament.[36] The election was a great step in the transformation of Bangladesh from military dictatorship to a civilian rule. But, even after election the rule remained authoritarian under the cover of civilianisation. It was also termed as Zia's 'Martial Democracy.'

On April 6, 1979, Zia Announced the withdrawal of martial law and stated, "Let us forget all difference and engage ourselves sincerely in the national reconstruction, irrespective of race, religion and party and march towards the desired goal for building a happy, prosperous and democratic country."[37]

The opposition political parties[38] in Bangladesh dur-

---

33. Quoted in M.Q. Zaman, Op.cit, p. 199.

34. Ibid.

35. Veena Kukreja, Op.cit, p. 168.

36. M.Q. Zaman, Op.cit. p. 200.

37. See Appendix-IV, For Full text of Zia's address to nation.

38. S.R. Chakravarty, "Bangladesh Survey of Domestic Scene," South Asian Studies. Vol. XII, No. 182, July-Dec. 1977. P. 65.

ing Zia's regime consisted of Awami League, Communists Party of Bangladesh, floated rightists, National Awami Party, Jatiya Samajtantrik Dal and a few newly emerged parties like, Bangladesh Democratic League of Khodkar Mushtaq Ahmed; Bangladesh Jatiya Janta Party of M.A.O.G. O and many others.

The pro-government political parties[39] included national Awami Party (Bhashini) (NAP (B)), Maoist Parties, Islam Pasand Parties and a few newly floated parties. However, under the situations of chaos and confusion prevailing in the country, the B.N.P. suffered internal dissension. The diverse elements in the B.N.P. also started working outside the party. "Lobbying, counter lobbying, gathering around certain leaders, the use of musclemen on occasions, and conflicts among the front line organisations became regular features of the party activities. Some high ranking leaders started to rely more on musclemen than genuine party workers to demonstrate and to keep up their influence and power."[40]

The party system remained weak under the military rule. Parties were not well organised. But, Zia provided a greater opportunity for the oppositional parties to flourish, and to act in parliament. By showing that he believes in democratic norms. Zia gathered mass support. The parliament was posed as a legislative decision making authority, though not effective.

---

39. Ibid, p. 69.

40. Golam Hossain, From Military to Military : B.N.P's Persistent Factionalism and Failure of Civilian Succession in Bangladesh," South Asian Studies Vol. XXI, No. 1, Jan, 1986, p. 66.

under zia regime, the bureaucrats emerged as a political force in the governing of the country. The bureaucracy, in fact shared power with military. The planning commission was reorganised with the bureaucrats occupying the important positions. In all public organisations, the generalists manned the top positions, and in field administration, members of the erstwhile generalist services held the much sought after posts of commissioner of deputy commissioner as the chief coordinators, with immense power and prestige in the districts and divisions. Weilding such enormous powers, these bureaucrats were able to scrap all laws that were made by Mujib regime to control the public servants. They were in charge of their own career management and thus formulated rulers that ensured their continued advancement in the governmental hierarchy. Even after the restoration of political activity in country in 1978 and the return of people's representatives through general elections in early 1979, the bureaucratic elites continued to act as statesmen in disguise favouring the political superiors. Thus, the major institution of bureaucracy i.e. the military bureaucratic model which appeared, hampered the growth of democratic institutions.

Although the bureaucracy in Bangladesh as a whole emerged triumphant in the second half of the 1970s in its struggle for greater power and authority in the political system, its internal dynamics tore it as under.

The bueraucrats inherited an authoritarian attitude as a legacy under British and Pakistan regimes. Most of the bueraucrats had their past experiences during Martial law regimes of Pakistan. "The bueraucrats who represented middle class in Pakistan had name to occupy an upper class in Bangladesh. The Bengali civil servants came from 'a low occupational status' and from 'low income groups'. But in Bangladesh they represented the higher strata of the society, along with the landowners, emerging businessmen and insustrial elites, professionals and government servants. In terms of income status and power they came at the top of the society. The bent of bureaucracy of Bangladesh was, thus, towards authoritarianism. Over time, new alignments or realignments took place and an entirely new pattern emerged."[41] The earlier factions were replaced by another set of microbureaucracies / interest groups with distinct features, memberships and group values. Some, even with under fined boundaries and thereby overlapping, but with conflicting objectives. Each of the groups considered itself a self contained entity and looked upon the others as competitors. Those public servants charged with the performance of pure administrative functions were divided into two groups, the ex PCS (ex-Pakistan Civil Service) and the ex-EPCSs (Ex-East Pakistan Civil Services) each antagonistic to the other although apparently manifesting togetherness.

"Those involved in the performance of specific function in the audit or accounts branches, customs, exise, police, taxation and other departments had their respective alignments and were opposed to be the administrative group which they believed acted against their interests. Finally, the technocrats-were grouped together in specific categories with the promotion of their own values and goals

41. Khan and Zafarullah, "Public Bureaucracy in Bangladesh," in K.K. Tummala (ed.) Administrative Systems Abroad. (Washington : University Press of America, 1982), p. 162.

in contradiction to those of the chaos characterised by frequent strikes or stop-work intervals in government departments and continuous mudslinging among the interest groups.[42] All this precipitated a crises; with the regime loosing control of the situation and forced by the craft of the unassailable bureaucrats into compromise and concession. Interansigence won over indifference, with the bureaucracy becoming a force to be reckoned with. The development strategies under zia were also in the interest of bureaucracy. During his regime, the civil-military bueraucrats formed an alliance-a'marriage of convenience,'

"and were continously dominant in the main decision making structures of the state apparatus (the office of the president, the cabinet, the National Economic Council (NEC), the Planning Commission, the public corporations etc.) which were formerly dominated by political elites during the 1972-75 regime of Sheikh Mujibur Rahman. Although zia formed a political p latform t hrough the Bangladesh Nationalist Party (BNP), and there was an elected parliament, the bureaucrats were the main decision-maders inthe sense that parliamnent was not a soverign body. It was subservience to the president who was a nominee of armed forces."[43]

So during his regime state interventionist measures weighted in favour of the hegemony of the ruling class.

---

42. Habib Mohammad Zafarullah, "Public Administration in the First Decade of Bangladesh," Asian Survey, Vol XXVIII, No. 4, April, 1987, p, 470.

43. Syed Serajul Islam, "Relative State Autonomy and Development Strategies in Bangladesh, 1975-81, "Pacific Affairs, Vol. LIX, No. 4, Winter, 1986-87, p. 563.

The economic role of the state was modelled on specific acts of regulation, corresponding the situations and interests; and through a process related with the nature of such regulation, the power to fix and enact rulers had shifted from the parliament towards executive. This caused decline in parliamentary system. State came under the dominating classes. As a result, the place of political parties had declined and undergone transformation. The state administration supported by the executive blocked the access channel formerly open to the political parties as representatives of the masses and thus assumed the role of guardians through imposition of authority and repression. In the rural areas also the administration was reluctant to share power with the political parties. On the other hand, the political content of the various state functions was geared to the continuance of the hegemony of power relations. "The constituated institutional apparatuses of the state englufed both the local level institutions and the central level institutions giving direct role to the latter (dominated by military-bureaucratic apparatus)."[44]

Zia undertook many reforms for rural development. But before these reforms could have any inpact, another military intervention in Bangladesh politics led to their termination. The political system moving towards liberal democratic objectives was thrown back into the dungeon of a military dictatorship. Zia's policies of over democratistion made some of the military personnel unhappy as they wanted to play an active role in political decision making processes. Dissatification among some

---

44. Comilla and U.J., A Comparative Stuy of Rural Development Politics, (Dacca : Centre for Social Studies, 1981). p. 47.

military personnel resulted in a coup of 1981. The coup was thus, of Corporate nature.

The violent end of zia in the abortive military coup was followed by the constitutionlly elected government of Justice Abdus Sattar. Although, the army leadership had backed Sattar and the B.N.P., it was far from satisfied with the party, Political confusion increased when on Feb. 11, 1982, President sattar dismissed the entire dismissed the entire cabined and reconstructed it, after sacking 22 ministers for alleged corruptions and incompetance. It was reported that military exerted pressure on the President to take this action.[45]

Ershad wanted constitutional provisions and administrative measures to define clearly the role of the military in Bangladesh society. He stated that "armed forces stand for democratic and constitutional process. They only watn to be with people to help build democracy, help build effective checks and balances against any future coup attempts."[46] Emphasizing on politico-military problems he said, "what is important is the fundamental concept of recognising the politico-military problems and finding permanent solutions through constitutional approach."[47] On the role of armed forces he said,

"Our military is an efficient, well disciplined, most honest body of truly dedicated and organised, national

---

45. Quoted in M. Rashiduzzaman in "Bangladesh Today," Current History. Vol LXXXI, No. 475, May 1982, p. 208.

46. See Appendix-IV for text of Ershad's speech on assigning constitutional role to the armed forces.

47. Ibid.

force. Potentials of such an excellent force in a poor country like ours can be effectively untilised for productive and nation-building purpose in addition to its role in national defence."[48]

From the statements the ideological orientation of military to take part in politics of the country is confirmed. Armed forces were to be utilised for nation building purposes and for socialisation. Nation building was taken as a part of military's national defence programme.

But, before any constitutional provisions could be made, the army under Ershad's leadership on March 24, 1982 took over direct and complete control of the country. The bloodless coup was not unexpected as the civilian government's ability to stop corruption and manage the economy and the law and order situation had steadily deteriorated.

Military internvention was a serious blow to the democratic institutions as it replaced a democratically elected government, Ershad, however, justified the coup by declaring that the introduction of the Martial Law in the country had been dictated by the aim to prevent a complete collapse of the economy, to end the in-effective functioning of the civil administration and the prevalence of corruption at all levels of power, to re-establish law and order and to maintain the national independance and sovereignty of Bangladesh. In his words, the Government of Abdus Sattar, "Had plunged the country into a situation of extreme hopelessness, desparation and uncertainty, which forced the army to take power for the sake of saving Bangladesh from a social, adminstrative and economic

---

48. Ibid.

catastrope."[49] Military intervention was justified as to save the country from acarchy, chaos, corruption and underdevelopment, though from previous military rule it had become clear that even military can no eradicate these problems.

Ershad stressed on the role of armed forces in the political institutions. Edplaining this, one of President Ershad's Principal Staff Officer, a Maj. Gen, said,

"The armed forces are patriots and also the best and well organised institutions in the country, what's the harm if we, with our training, expertize and infrastructure also help in running the country? Why should we be left out? After all the country's are weak disorganised and ill-equiped to shoulder this onerous responsibility. Past experience bears ample testimony to this," with a note of caution he added, "Don't forget that two Presidents were assassinated for keeping the military out of power. if it is wronged again, the army will continue to be the source of destablization."[50] Military assumed new role in developing world, quite different from that of the developed.

Ershad, like zia, tried to civilianize through various reforms,[51] in order to legitimize his rule. First related to changes in political and bureaucratic role allocations in local government, i.e. a move from bureaucracy towards democracy. Secondly, the upzila parishad was granted the status of executive agency increasing its responsibility,

---

49. See Appendix-VI & VII. For full detail of texts of proclamation of Martial law and Ershad's views.

50. Manash Ghosh, "Bangladesh Today-II : Is the Army Indispensable? The Statesman (editorial), Jan. 16, 1984., p. 4.

and decreasing parliamentry democracy. Thirdly, Ershad's reforms provided for a redefination os inter-bureaucratic relationships in local government.

Ershad also emphasised on the process of decentralisation. "The process of administrative and governmental decentralisation involved major changes in both the structure of central government personel posted in rural communities and in roles played by local governments in making resource allocation decisions."[52] Thus, decentralisation gave rise to many conflicts, as it was a move to control the bureaucrats.

"Gen. Ershad while civilianizaing his process followed Bangladesh variety of presidential referendum, election of local bodies (upzila Parishads, parliamentary and presidential elections) after partially reviving the constitution, and amending the representation of people order (1972) and off and on banning political activities, arresting political leaders and so on. Failure of the Junta to curb corruption or lay the fundation of economic infrastructure intensified social unrest. But distribution of favours in various forms enabled him to legalise all proclamation orders, C.M.L.A.'s orders, Martial law regulation, Martial law orders and Martial law instructions. These were reported by the prociamation of withdraw of Martial Law on November 10, 1986. The constitution was revived fully. But his aims of Islamisation and of constitutionally

---

51. See; Nizam Ahmed, "Experiments in Local Goverment Reform in Bangladesh," Asian Survey Vol. XXVIII, no. 8, August, 1988, pp. 821-829.

52. Ibid. p. 825.

guranteed role for military in the political system remained unfulfilled."[53]

In order to remain in power he devised means to divide the existing political parties including the largest two- The B.N.P. and A.L. in which one faction sided with him. Gen. Ershad formed "Nutan Bangla Jubo Sanghati (New Bangla Youth Solidarity) and Natun Bangla Chatra Samaj (New Bangal Students Association). Which later on became the youth and student's wing of the government backed 'Janadal' (People's Party). Ershad, However, did not join 'Janadal'. Jandal was conglomeration of diverse elements of splinter groups and parties. Ershad took further steps to form a broader political platform by forming 'National Front' comprising Janadal, one faction of each Muslim league, united people's party, B.N.P. and a few individuals. As a result of all this 'Jatiya Party' came into existence in January, 1986. It indicated that Ershad civilianised his rule through Jatiya Party (J.P.). Zia-ur-Rahman patronized the B.N.P. party and similarly Ershad patronized the J.P. Both the parties were the result of the conglomeration of opportunistic elements and lacked ideological orientation. These parties were thus, only the instruments for legitimising their rules. There is marked similiarity in the strategies, tactics, and ideology of both the military rulers. This similiarity, however, can be percieved in most of the military rulers of developing countries, where identity and resource mobilisation crisis can be manipulated for legitimizing military rule.

The main opposition to the administration of Ershad was constituted on one hand, by the union of 15 left and

53. Ibid. p. 864.

democratic parties which consisted of the Awami League, the communist party of Bangladesh, the national Awami Party, the Jatiya Samaj Tantrik Dal, the Workers party, the Samyabadi Dal and a number of other smaller political organisations, and on the other hand, there was an alliance of seven rightwing and conservative parties, which had grouped around the nationalist party led by Zia-ur-Rahman's widow Khaleda zia. Both the opposition blocks acted in a parallel manner and to a certain extent coordinated their actions.[55] The opposition political parties were themselves faction ridden. A.L. the major component of 15 party alliance got divided and one faction was now called BAKSAL (Bangladesh Krishak Shramik Awami League.)

These internal dissentions among the parties helped Ershad to consolidate his rule by divide and rule tactics. The unorganised party system, thus helped military to play effective role in politics. In order to have the appraisal of military's policies and to show the legitimacy of his government, Ershad held a referendrum. "In a countrywide referendum on March 21, 1985 under a tightened martial law administration. Gen. Ershad secured 94% of the 51% voted cast, which was interpreted as a massive vote of confidence in his leadership, polices and programmes."[56]

Although the constitution was not followed in its strict sense, but in order to legitimise his role, Ershad proposed the constitution's 8th amendment act (1988) in May, which

---

54. Bangladesh Observer, Jan. 13, 1986.

55. V.P. Puchkov, Political Development in Bangladesh : 1971-85, (New Delhi : Partiot Publishers, 1989), p. 193.

56. Bangladesh Observer, March 23, 1985

"introduced a new article (2A) that declared Islam to be the state religion of Bangladesh, but stated that other religions could be freely practised, The bill also amended article 100 allowing the government to decentralise the judicial system and set up six permanent benches of the high court division of the supreme court."[57] This bill passed in June, 1988, factionalised the oppositin groups on the issue of religion.

But, by now it had become clear that without a common effort of all political parties, it was difficult to dislodge Ershad from his power. In a meeting held between the two opposition leaders i.e., Begam Khaleda Zia and Sheikh Hasina, they agreed on a common strategy to oust the military government.[58] In order to force the government to resign, the opposition drew up the plans of strikes and demonstrations. Sheikh Hasina said "if Ershad fails to quit, the people will bring everything barring transport to a complete stand still on November 10, 1987."[59] While in March, 1988, Ershad was contesting the presidential election as a nominee of J.P. and claimed that he enjoyed the support, the opposition denounced it as a 'farcical' election and boycotted the poll. "After the major opposition parties boycotted the elections, President Ershad compounded his problems by enacting the force of getting together a motely group of splinter parties and grouping to contest them, Further, he maintained his schedule by en-

57. Syedur Rahman, "Bangladesh in 1988 : Precarious Institution Building Amid Crisis Management," Asian Survey Vol. XXIX, No. 2, Feb., 1989, p. 218.

58. Hindustan Times, March 12, 1986.

59. The Hindu, Nov. 8, 1987.

couraging widespread rigging to be able to claim a great victory for his Jatiya party on the basis of a 50% turn out. Independent witness suggested a turnout of not more than 5%, although opposition spokesmen suggested that it was one percent."[60]

During Ershad's regime, the political activity took the 'form of indoor politics.' i.e. 'no public outdoor meetings were held. The political decision could be taken in the privacy of homes or party offices. The press carried reports about the activities of major organisations and even of the almost countless tiny groups that described themselves as parties. At times, political leaders and their followers had been subject to detention, but major personalities had usually been detained only brielfy and had often been placed under house arrest rather than jail arrest. Perhaps the main reason for house arrest was that the leaders of two groups opposing Ershad were women.'[61]

During Ershad regime bueraucracy was subordinate to military. Under his autocratic regime the attempts were made for the destruction of all values, norms and institutions of democracy. All the civil and military authority was concentrated in one person. There were indisputable evidences of the infringement on parliament's authority as the sovereign in the legislative process. Other institutions were also feeble. It was the highest degree of concentration of power with which he ruled the country for

---

60. Nihal Singh, "Logic of Military Rule Tragedy of Bangladesh," The Times of India, March 22, 1988.

61. Craig Baxter, "Continuing Problems in Bangladesh, "Current History", Vol. LXXXII, No. 509, March 1986, p. 122.

nine years without any checks and balances against the exercies of his personal wishes. As the formal political institutions had been made competely ineffective, it was the mass movement which succeded at a last removing him from the platform. "Before the October-November, 1990 events that led to the fall of Ershad, Bangladesh's internal politics were dominated by the familiar themes of factionalism with in Ershad's Jatiya Party (J.P.), the rivalries between and the Bangladesh Nationalist Party (B.N.P.)-dominated seven-party alliance and threats of a hartal."[62]

J.P. was not clearly united party although all groups within it pledged loyality to Ershad. The emergence of the parties such as B.N.P. and Awami League was a positive move towards democracy. The mass upsurge forced Ershad to resign. The chief justice of Supreme Court, Justice Shahabuddin Ahmed was given a mandate by all opposition political parties to hold free and fair elections of the Jatiya Sangsad within three months of his assuming office. Thus, the society prevailed over armed section of the state.

Before elections a hectic political drama was staged, manifesting itself in various forms and alliances and counter alliances, allegations and personal charisma. The election process began to represent a political tussel between the eight party alliance of Awami League under Sheikh Hasina Wajed and seven party alliance of (B.N.P.) under Begam Zia. Apart from these there were two major

---

62. Craig Baxter, "Bangladesh in 1990 : Another New Beginning," 'Asian Survey' Vol. XXXI, No. 2, Feb. 1991, p. 146.

parties in the fray-j.p. led by Gen. Ershad and the right-wing Jamait-i-Islami. "There were 108 political parties registered with the election commission of Bangladesh."[63]

In the political compaigns Khaleda Zia emphasised on the impermentation of Zia's 19-point programme. She upheld the islamic provisions in the Constitution during zia regime. She criticised A.L. rule of Mujib and accused Ershad of destroying democratic political institutions. Sheikh Mujib was the main theme of Sheikh Hasina's campaign. She promised for a living secular democracy and denounced the military rules of zia and Ershad who used Islam to increase their appeal to people.

Elections were held on Feb. 27, 1991. Elections were held in free and fair atmosphere. "The B.N.P. won 140 of the 300 seats; the A.L. won 88 seats and its allies 11. In a mild surprise J.P. of Ershad won 35 seats, JI won 18, which offered to the B.N.P. to permit to have an absolute majority."[64]

The country now had a democratically elected government. Businessmen and industrialist class came to hold the reigns of power. Khaleda zia was sworn in as Prime Minister on March 19, 1991 and switched over to parliamentry democracy on September 19, 1991. In order

---

63. Muzaffar Hussain, "Rivalry Between Hasina and Khaleda will determine the failure of Bangladesh," Organiser, Jan. 20, 1991, p. 11.

64. Craig Baxter and Syedur Rehman, "Bangladesh Votes 1991-Building Democratic Institution." Asian Survey Vol. XXXI, No. 8, Aug. 1991, p. 687.

to keep military out of assuming political role Begam Zia emphasised on building democratic political institutions to cope with the demands of the people.

Bangladesh has been oscillating between the democratic and military leaderships. The internal crisis has potentially undermined the development processes and the national stability. This is also attributed to weak political institutions, which are unable to instill law and order in the society. Because of uncertainties of the capablities of political institutions and deteriorating scene in the heading of various situations emerges and ultimately leads to political instability. The un evolved democratic institutions leads the authorization tendencies to creep in, as the concentration of power comes in few hands in the absence of clear division of responsibilities. Even after the elections of 1991, 1996, 2001 the instability remains the area of concern. Even during 2001 elections, the care taker government headed by Justice Latifur Rahman initiated a beaurocratic procedure for separation of judiciary from executive, the ordinance too was issued by the President Ahmed Shahabuddin, but without much success. The office of executive too is no immune to the over powering execution. "On june 21, 2002 the ruling B.N.P alliance asked Badarudoza Chawdhary to step down for not showing sufficient 'deference' to the B.N.P founder general Ziaur Rahman, as to declare Bangladesh independence." The absence of strong institutional checks and balances within the democratic process.

The tenure of Begum Khaleda Zia ended on 28th October, 2006 and pretrial Iajuddin Ahmad took over the challenges for the new President.

Meanwhile, H.M. Ershad also returned to active politics in september, 2006, demanding withdrawal of pending cases against institutions. In late October, 2006, Bangladesh faced political deadlock with B.N.P Khaled Zia Awami league (major political alliance) pressurizing for electoral reforms. Nearly 70 people were killed and hundreds injured in the agitation lead by AL-alliance, which continued till January, 2007 parliamentary elections and subsequently withdrew all its candidates. A.L. charged B.N.P with capturing/dominating on various seats by unlawful manner in the absence of equal opportunities on free and fair elections.

The election boycott lead to constitutional crises and once again opened the doors for a possible army take over. As per the circumstances president Iajuddin Ahmed signed for the part of chief administration on 11th Jan 2007 and declared a state emergency across the country.

The new care taker government expressed commitment to free the politics from criminal activities and reform electoral processes and to do away with 'black money' and 'muscle power' People and media welcomed the views expressed by the caretaker government. But in July, 2007 the media expressed concern about the arrest of Khaleda Zia and Sheikh Hasina on the charges of corruption.

"Bangladesh ranks 19th as among weak and falling states. It scores a high of 9 in criminalisation and delegitimisation of state. It ranks 156 on corruption perception index (CPI) 2006." (Source : Survey Indices/CPI/2006)

The President, Fakhruddin Ahmed has vowed to cleanse the country of corruption before holding polls towards the end of 2008.

As far as India-Bangladesh ties are concerned, insurgency problem remains an irritant. In lack of democratic institutions the bilateral talks get a setback. Setting of border disputes also remains an area of concern in the lack of, "intelligence sharing, joint inspections, re-habilitation of desplaced."

The politics of dissent have also started getting place amongst various political parties as the reform plans are being made. They are aiming that the same prime ministers should not come to power again. The interim government is restriction activity to few chosen people, putting/imposing restrictions on the rest. According to Begum Khaleda Zia, "The process of on-going reforms in political parties would create suspicion among people---the country needs, not only structural changes in political parties, it also needs reforms in overall political culture."

Form the above account, it is clear that the military intervenes in the societies which have low institutional growth. In the views of Michal Kalecki, "the societies marked by the absence of a well developed industrial captialist establishment allied to a big landord class, What he called as 'intermediate classes' tend to exercise state power for their own advantage. And in this they allien themselves to various groupings such as civil bureaucracy, military and civil politicians ans also rich peasants, the elities,"[65] the same happened in the polity of Bangladesh.

---

65. Michal Kalecki, "Social and Economic Aspects of Intermediate Regimes," in his Selected Essays on the Economic Growth of the Social and Mixed Economy, (Cambridge : Cambridge University Press, 1972), pp. 162-169.

Under the influential work of Huntington, it is a easy to characterise the Bangladesh political system as 'praetorian i.e. with low levels of institutionalisation and high level of participation. As the institutions of civil and military bueraucracies were more highly developed than the political parties, military had strong, incentives to move into institutional vacuum on the input side of political system and to attempt to perform interest aggregate functions. The rise of democracy, once again, in the developing countries and particularly in Bangladesh can be analysed in the context of failure of military's performance in institutionalisation under the rising era of expectations.

The presence of unorganised political parties with no particular ideology and lack of mass base made the democratic practice under strain. The disposition of intolerance towards opposition parties also proved to be a big hurdle.

There were no well organised pressure groups which could mobilise the public towards democratic policies and thus military had to face no such resistance while coming into politics.

Even the political culture was characterised by structural fragmentation, fomenting atomisation of individual economic interests. Even poor people tried to maximise their economic goals by attaching themselves to persons who were powerful and prestigious, such political mobilisation helped in encouraging the non-democratic institutions. The institution building processes didn't work well in the polity of Bangladesh, The political institutions lacked the virtues of complexity, autonomy and adaptability.

Thus, the army intervened into the politics of

Bangladesh when there were democratic political institutions, weak political parties, no pressures groups and weak political culture. All these factors which in a way helped army to take part in active politics were never allowed to flourish by the military rulers as they considered that these factors could put a challange to their regimes. The presence of identity, resource mobilisation, penetration, and distribution crisis also helped military to come into the politics. The political and governmental institutions do not operate in vacuum, they are affected by the prevailing socio-economic conditions in the society. Hence, the study of enviromental variables as factors for enhancing or retarding the role of military in politics would be incomplete without dealing with the socio-economic coditions. Therefore, in the ensuing chapter an attempt has been made to evolve the relationship of military vis-a-vis socio-economic modernisation of Bangladesh.

V-Military and Socio-economic Modernisation

Military's intervention into politics is conditioned by prevailing environmental factors. Apart from political institutions, socio-economic structures are also the important basis of environmental variables. Miliatary does not operate in the vacuum but it is a part of an overall socio-economic structure. It's behaviour is actually conditioned by wide socio-political and socio-ectonomic processes. Thus, socio-economic conditions are the factors which inhance or inhibit the role of military in politics.

Military steps into the political arena of the country in order to restore political stablity and to imporve socio-economic condition acting as a modernising agent. As Ershad himself has expressed, military steps in, "where a situation arises in the country in which economic life is in a position of collapse, the civil administration unable to effectively function, wanton corruption at all levels permissible part of life causing unbearable suffering to the people... where the people of the country are plunged into a state of extreme frustration, despair and uncertainty."[1] Military, thus, assumes the role of nation building in addition to national defence. But, if military is un-

---

1. From Text of Ershad's speech.

able to deal effectively with severe socio-economic crises-violent malpractics, rampant corruptions and does social justice, it adds to the frustration of the masses because their expections are not met with. Such frustrations result in coups and counter-coups and transitions to democracy.

The socio-economic conditions are motivatiors for social and political changes since there is constant interplay between the social structure and the development of political elites in a given society. The socio-economic and socio-political potentiabls and configurations of a society are, thus, related to military's intervention in politics.

Deteriorated socio-economic conditions which Bangladesh inherited form the two colonoal rules helped military to play an active role in its political sphere.

Bangladesh, at the time of independence, had shattered economy, high amount of poverty and illiteracy and formidable economic and political problems, which were beyond solution.

In predominetly rural society of Bangladesh, about 91% of people lived in rural areas, and 77% of them depended on agriculture.[2] Since land is the chief means of production in rural areas, inequalities stement primarily from skewed distribution of land ownership. The basic mass of the Bangladesh rural population consisted of poor peasant households. According to official figures, in the mid-seventies out of 11,849,000 families living in the rural areas 1,312,000 (11.1%) were completely landless and

2. Talukder Maniruzzaman, "The Future of Bangladesh," in A Jeyratnam, Wilson and Dannis Daltons' "The States of South Asia" (New Delhi : Vikas publishing House, 1982), p. 272.

5,621,000 (47.4%) owned tiny plots of land of upto one acre in area. To their share fell only 9.7% of the total land stock of the country.[3] A considerable part of the most deprived mass of the rural population, thus, belonged to the agricultural labour. The other part was engaged in small handicrafts, fishing, water transport, construction work etc., These classes had no socio-economic power to play in the society and were not much attached to the political activities of the state and formed low political culture viable for military's intervention.

According to data provided by Bangladesh scholars, "62.4% of the urban and 71.3% of the rural population lived below poverty line. The average per capita income in 1969-70 was only 450 taka (62 dollars), which was lowest in the world.[4] 59% of the population did not get its diet, a sufficient number of calories and more than 80% suffered from a great inefficiency of vitamines.[5]

In Bangladesh society, at horizontal level there were cleavages between rural and urban areas and at the verticle level between rich and poor. With the abolition of landlordism and large scale departure of Hindu landed interests, a class of surplus farmers known as Jotedars, emerged as most powerful exploiting element in rural Bangladesh. By virtue of their socio-economic power, the jotedars

---

3. Statistical Year book of Bangladesh Bureau of Statistics, Government of People's Republic of Bangladesh, Dhaka, 1979, p. 144-45.

4. Quted in V.P. Puckhov,Political Development of Bangladesh 1971-85, (New Delhi : Patriot Publishers, 1989), p. 19.

5. Ibid.

monopolised in the modern agricultural inputs. Consequently, the Jotedars made profit, purchased more and more land which resulted in class polarisation, marginalisation and proletarianization of the rural masses.

At the top of the Bangladesh village, was the stratum of landlords (according to official sources there were only 96,000 or 0.8% of the families) each of whom owned landed property of over 15 acres in area, a total of 2,184,000 acres. It was this stratum which exercised economic and political power in the village and even in the country. Two thirds representative organs of self government the rural councils belonged to this top stratum. More than half of the members of Bangladesh national assembly elected in 1973 were landlords owning fifteen or more acres of land.[6] This dominant class had good representation in military recruitment too which later played a political role.

The middle classes who often shared power and privileges eith ruling elite emerged as most powerful elements of exploitation in Bangladesh social formation. Their interests were protected by bureaucrated military oligarchy. The middle class in Bangladesh was very articulate, cohesive and organised and played a significant role in socio-economic and political life of Bangladesh

The middle classes mainly included employees and intelligentia. They constitued a numers stratum of Bangladesh society. The intelligentia was a very big dy

6. V.P. Puchkov, Op. cit. p 24.

namic element in the social stratum of Bangladesh. Among the intelligentsia majority were teachers. The development of the system of education led to a rapid growth in the number of intelligentia. They were mainly drawn from the more prosperous part of the population. With the emergence of such a class in the society of Bangladesh, With the emergence of such a class in the society of Bangladesh, which became aware of the political tactics of the rulers, When ever there was decline in socio-economic conditions or their intersts were thretened they actively conditions or their intersts were thretened they actively poted for a change of rule whether it was civilian or military. The social structure of Bangladesh in a transitional stage from the colonoal feudal society to bourgeoies society encouraged development of money commodity relations in the village population leading to a considerable expansion of the proletarian and semi-proletarian masses.

On the eve of the achievement of the independence, the working class accounted for 976,000 persons of whom 403,000 were engaged in the modern sectors of industry. The strongest contingent of the proletariat belonged to workers of the jute mills - 192,000 persons. A large number of workers i.e. 287,000 persons were concentrated in the three chief industrial sector-Dhaka, Naryanganj, Chittagong and Khulana.[7]

The Bangli bourgeoisie which sided with Mujib in liberation war owned 34 out of 68 jute mills working in the country, 24 textile mills (out of 45), 16 companies exporting jute, 12 shipping and 12 exporting companies and

7. Ibid. p. 25.

so on. However, about 168 Bengal companies had collaboration with Pakistan.[8] Most of the capitalists sided with Awami league in order to seek their private interestes. But, later on as some of the radicalist elements in Awami league pressed for socialistic economic order, the capitalists started malpractices. They started corrupting thef system in order to gain private interests. Such tendencies on the one hand imbibed corruption in political spheres which weakened the political base and, on the other hand, it resulted in deteriorating socio-economic conditions. Both the factors ultimately, called for the military's active role in politics.

During Mujib regime the bureaucratic elite were not held in high esteem because of their associations with the military rule in Pakistan during the last 12 years. These bureaucratic elites were deprived of their privileges during Mujib regime. Only the Awami league politicians dominated the social and political scene. All these politicians had no experience of administration hence, they failed to implement the policies framed by the government, this further resulted in deteriorating the socio-economic conditions. The members of Mujib's cabinet came from different fields of socio-economic strata and only two were professional politicians. (See Table :1)

---

8. Ibid. p. 28.

Table-1

Socio-economic Background of Mujib's Cabined Members:[9]

Profession	Number
Lawyers	13
Business executive	4
Jotedar	1
Teacher	1
Labour	1
Military	1
Professional Politician	2

The economic situation in the country continued to be critical. This was partly due to the global inflation which hit the wolds in 1972 and partly due to inefficiency and corruption of the workers of Awami League (A.L.), "Mujib appointed untrained politicians in the economic Management and administration having distrust on civil-military bureaucracy. Production as a result declined to an unusually low level in the nationalised sector. Though the government nationalised more than 87% of the foreign trade, the distribution of the imported goods was made through licenced delaers, Most of the licencees were the Awami league workers and they became the owners of large sums

9. Sayed Serajul Islam, "Nature of Regime and Leadership in Bangladesh (1972-73)," Seminar Procedings, Bangladesh Political Science Association, 1985, p. 12.

of unearned money."[10] The corruption, thus, prevailed in every sphere, which weakened the political system.

The economy was at the verge of collapse by the middle of 1974 due to the sharp decline of production, large scale smuggling and natural disaster. The soaring price level of basic consumer goods, decline of production in the nationalised sector, widespread corruption led to unstable socio-economic condition.

"During one year (May 72-May73) 372 cases of murder, armed robberies and burgalaries occured and the increase over the previous year was 300 % for armed robberies, 900% for burgalaries and 200% for smuggling."[11] It was estimated that about 6000 persons in Bangladesh were killed for political reasons since independence."[12] And, according to an official estimate of the total value of goods smuggled out of Bangladesh between January 1972 and August 1975 was $ 4 billion (Tk 60 billion).[13] These formative years of Bangladesh were chaotic and anarchic though there was presence of charismatic leadership of Sheikh Mujibur Rahman.

"The production during Mujib regime remained below the 1969-70 level. The per capita income declined. More than half the industrial capacity remained unutilised.

---

10. Emajuddin Ahmed, "Military Rule and the Mvth of Democracy," (Dhaka : University Press Limited, 1988), p. 59.

11. Morning News, Dhaka, Aug 16, 1973, p. 3.

12. Ibid, Nov. 5, 1973, p. 2

13. W.B. Reddaway and Md. Mizahur Rahman, "The Scale of Smuggling out in Bangladesh," Economic and Political Weekly, June 5, 1976, p. 843.

Polutaion expended at the rate of 0.2 milliaon a year and the annual food deficit varied between 10% to 30 % of the requirement. The 600odd industrial units taken over by state were not in good health. An investment of Tk. 1400 crores under first five year plan started in July, 1973 made little difference."[14] Bangladesh got the world sympathy and remained a testing groung for the programmes of world bank and other international agencies.

Table-2

Total Imports and Exports[15] During Mujib Regime

Year	Total Imports (million dollars)	Total Exports (million dollers)
1973	986	358
1974	1078	348
1975	1321	327

The Table indicates that the exports went on decreasing and imports kept on increasing, affecting the economy of the country adversely.

As, the economic conditions continued to deteriorate the prices of essential goods rose by 300% to 400%

14. G.P. Deshpande, Bangladesh : The Gods that failed Democratic World, 1976, Vol. V, No. 3, Jan 18, 1976, p. 9.

15. World Military Expenditure and Arms Transfer, (Washington : U.S. Arms Control and Disarmament, 1985), p. 96.

over the 1969-70 level.[16] Increasing inflationary pressures on the economy since 1972, mainly due to general rise of prices in international markets further affected at large the rural poor. Thus the resulting pauperisation led to an unprecedented concentration of extreme poverty. According to one estimate, "back in 1963-64 about 40 percent of the rural population lived below the absolute poverty line. By 1975-75, the percentage had gone upto 62 percent. About 5 percent of rural people were below the extreme poverty line in 1963-64, but the percentage rose to 40 percent in 1974-75."[17]

As the economy of the country virtually collapsed, the government desperately needed foreign aid. Bangladesh recevied about 400 million dollars in the cash and kind as emergency assistance and about 145 million dollar as loan from various countries and international organisations.[18]

Apart from the social and economic crisis Mujib had to face the uprisings of Chittagong Hill Tracts who had organised themselves against the Dacca government and formed a millitary front named 'Shanti Bahini', they felt that they were not getting proper economic incentives. In order to consolidate his polition, Mujib through a numbers of amendements started shifting from a democrat to an autocrat.

Mujibur Rahman, It seemed, was unable to grasp the realities of the situation and to handle the post-revolutionery society. Under his regime the society faced

---

16. Talukder Maniruzzaman, Group Interests and Political Changes : Studies in Pakistan and Bangladesh. (New Delhi : South Asian Publishers, 1982), p. 128.

17. Ibid. p. 228.

uncontrolable corruption, violence and factionalism. Uncontrolled law and order situation gave rise to political instability. While poverty, illitracy and economy continued as before, the country became increasingly restless at the hands of Mujib. The leader who opted for democratic norms had destroyed them. frustration and despair affected every honest Bengali, several competent senior official and other member or the elites prefered to settle abroad. The father of the nation had already lost the mandate of heaven under the worsely affected socio-economic conditions. "The country became a case study in economic stagnation, social tensions and political violence. Price inflation acccelerated devaluation. As a result, the middle class found its prosperity crumbling and its goals receding. Though a few people including some close to the government, continued to do well."[19] The military was reacting increasingly of coupe (i.e. August 15, 1945, Nov 3, 1975 and Nov. 7, 1975), as there was no other alternative in the absence of well organised oppositional political parties and leadership.

Thus, under the unstable political and poor socio-economic situations the country became an easy prey for ambitious Generals. In the apparent untidiness of political life and the alow functioning of political processes, the military appeared to be a tidy setup which was able to move with speed and apparent efficiency. As the political government's stock fell in the eyes of people, the armed

---

18. Ibid. p. 129.

19. B.K. Jahangir, "Nature of Class Struggle in Bangladesh," Economic and Political Weekly, Vol. XII, no. 50, Dec. 10, 1977, p.2.

forces appeared as an alternative. Weak democratic traditions could not prevent drift towards authoritarianism. The bureaucracy, claiming to be the natural rulers found it convenient to function behind the military sheild.

Military found it convinient to enter the politics of Bangladesh as it had taken an effecitve part in the liberation struggle (See Appendix-VII). Moreover, the active politicians of Awani League, the bureaucrats and military personnel were from the upper class. On the one hand, Mujib's radical policies threatened the interests of these upper and middle classes, on the other hand, their non-implementation had distanced him from the masses. The resentment of the public against the policies of Mujib and of army against the Mukti Bahini (a paramilitary force of Mujib) were also the main features which compelled military officers to coup.

The army in Bangladesh, in the guise of improving the prevailing socio-economic conditions, anarchy and chaos grabbed the political power and tried to maintain the status quo. Thus, Mujib was eliminated from the political scene and his radical polices were thwarted by army. Apparently army wanted to modernise the society. The groups which came to power after the August coup consisted of a coalition of forces, viz the rump of Awami League, the civil bureaucracy and the group of junior officers who had carried out the coup. This coalition however was not to last long, as the struggle for power in Bangladesh had no been resolved, especially among the upper echelons of army, moreover the junior officers who led the coup to do away with Mujibism had no socio-economic or socio-political the army resulted in coups and counter coups. And, ultimately Zia-ur-Rehman emerged as the strongst contingent of power.

With the military takeover, the bureaucracy smerged as a potent force in the governing of the country. The bureaucracy in fact, shared power with military. All in all during 1975-81 there was total reinstatement of bureaucratic power, largely due to the failure of the politicans in running the country. After coming into power, zia tried to telitimise his rule through elections and reforms. The economy was liberalised to some degree during his regime. In the economic policy he tried to use both private forces and state intervention.

The government discarded the socialistic pretensions of Mujib regime and took special measures to boost private foreign trade and private investment in industrial sector. He emphasised on export oriented industries, promoting a high rate of production. The primary goal of such a strategy was to maximise G.N.P. growth rate through all out encouragment of the private sector.[20] A ceiling of Taka 30 million fixed by the Mujib government for private investment was raised to Taka 100 million.[21] Private investment in industry increased from Taka 87.4 million in 1973-74 to Taka 2091. 4 million in 1977-78.[22] "During the period 1975-80, mearly thirty five thousand industrial units-mainly in the sectors of dairy farming and dairy products, deep sea fishing, agricultural machinery and equipment, readymade garments and drugs and pharmaceuticals

---

20. See Zia's address to the Dhaka Chamber of Commerce and Industries in August 1976 in The Bangladesh Observer. August 4, 1976, p. 4

21. Takukdar Maniruzzaman, Group Interests and Political Changes, Op. cit. p. 192.

ware approved by the investment board involving an investment of Taka. 4,407.4 milion. During the same period foreign investment also took place in thirty eight projects worth about $ 161 million. The foreign investment covered thirty eight joint ventures, fourteen of which were British Companies (U.S. $ 30 million) and three were American companies (U.S. $ 53 million).[23] Thus army's approach of socio-economic modernization was different from the political leaders. Army was in favour of liberalization of economy. Army revived the radical socialistic attitute towards socio-economic modernisation.

In this attempt to stablise the internal political situation, zia formulated a programme of action which expressed the basic directions of the work of this administration in the political and socio-economic fields, which came to be known as 19-point programme,[24] the greatest attention was paid to problems of an economic character, above all to the development of agriculture. The programme provided for the achievement of self sufficiency of the country in food production, giving the private sector the necessary incentives for the purpose of economic development of the country, prevention of a poupulation explosion, removal of illiteracy, decentralisation of the system of administration and de velopment and strengthening of local self-government. Zia

---

22. Government of People's Republic of Bangladesh, Planning Commission. The two Year Plan, 1978-80 (Dhaka, Government Press, 1968), p. 4.

23. S. Kamaluddin, "Bangladesh Lures the Investers," Far Eastern Economic Review, Nov. 23, 1979, p. 55.

24. See Bangladesh Times. Dhaka, May 1, 1977.

sought referendum on his 19-point programme with the aim of continuing his efforts for building up a happy and prosperous society for all.[25] About 19-point programme, he believed that, "it will strengthen the unity and solidarity of the country and guide it on the path of progress and prosperity."[26]

For the social upliftment, the government also launched a massive programme of manual digging and excavation of canals, and building of roads and embankment. By 1976, 2,200 miles of embankment and 900 miles of roads had been constructed and 2,200 miles of new canals excavated. In order to control population explosion, Zia's government appointed 12000 family planning officers through out the country to popularise the family planning programme.[27]

Efficient planning and implementation of polices resulted in marked improvements in all fields of Bangladesh's economy. Both the annual reports of the Bangladesh Bank and the World Bank 1975-76, revealed that Gross Domestic Product rose by 11-4 % in 1975-76, as against 2% in the preceding year. The overall cost of living index was estimated to have declined by 20% during the year as against a rise of 31% during 1974-75. Industrial output increased by 5% and, production of jute industry went up 7.3%. The export target fixed at the 5540 million in 1975-

25. For full text of speech see Appendix-II
26. Bangladesh Observer. June 4, 1977.

27. Talukder Maniruzzaman, "Group Interests and Political Changes," Op. cit. p. 192.

76 was exceeded by Tk. 560 million.[28]

In 1976-77, foreign trade showed little improvements. There were exports of 6211 million Taka and imports of 11,039 million Taka.[29] The exports increased by 48% over the corresponding year 1975-76.[30] However, the development of Bangladesh continued to depend on the extent of foreign aid. Bangladesh got a record total of about 1450 million dollars of foreign aid till 1976 as against 145 million dollars during Mujib regime.[31] In spite of huge amounts of foreign aid the socio-economic conditions showed nominal progress. "The practical stagnation in agriculture and industry, in spite of impressive assistance from abroad - which in 1978-79 was 1,857 million dollars, and the total of which in the period from December, 1971 to Jume 1979 was 7,972 million dollars aggravated the socio-economic problems of Bangladesh.[32] Prices of food, essential goods and services went up. Such socio-economic innditions showed decline in per capita income.

---

28. Ibid. p. 193.

29. Statistical Pocket Book of Bangladesh, (Dhaka : Bureau of Statistics, Government of People's Republic of Bangladesh, 1978), p. 14.

30. Takukder Maniruzzaman, Group Interests and Political Changes, op. cit. p. 193.

31. Ibid.

32. V.P. Puchkov, Op.cit. pp. 132-133.

Table-3

Per Capita Income (G.N.P.)[33]

	1972-73	1973-74	1974-75	1975-76	1976-77
Per Capita Income (G.N.P.) in Taka	584	891	1,574	1,261	1,208

The improvement of economy was temporary as massive foreign aid was flushed in Bangladesh. Hence later, results proved to be a set back self reliant economy of Bangladesh. Thus, it is difficult to say that military rule accelerates the socio-economic modernisation. The socio-economic variable does not fully explain the problem by itself without taking other variables into consideration. In fact, military rule tried to give lions share to military from the national cake. The defence budget had been revised upwards, which raised original allocation from the 750 million i.e. 7% of the national budget to Tk 1109.34 million, i.e. 20% of the national budget.[34] Just within two years of zia's takeover, defence and civil administration expenditures increased more than Tk. 2 billion, while all other budget categories 'conbined expenditure whith increased by less than Tk 1 billion.[35] The defence expendi

33. Statistical Pocket Book of Bangladesh, (Dhaka : Bureau of Statistics, Government of People's Republic of Bangladesh, 1978), p 239

34. Statistical Year Book of Bangladesh Op. cit. 1980, p. 363.

35. Mosharaf Hossain, "Nature of State Power in Bangladesh," Mainstream, Vol XVIII, No. 25-26, February 16-23, 1980, pp. 21-22.

ture increased during military regime of zia showed only a little of decline during his civilianisation process.

Government's development strategies were in fact the strategies to legitimise the military regime. The development strategy of zia was best suited for protecting the interests of indigenous bourgeoisie. The professional background of Zia's cabinet members shows that his civilinization process was a myth because, it was dominated by the military bureaucrats (table : 4). Hence, the lurking doubt remains wether that a military dictator could install a civilian regime. The civilianisation was also a strategy to legitimise the military rule by mobilising the civilian support. zia's last council of ministers also shows that military bureaucrats enjoyed the dominating position (Table : 5).

Table-4

President zia's Cabinet in April 1979[36]

Professional Background	Number
Military Bureaucrats	6
Civil Bureaucrats	2
Technocrats	8
Political Leaders	13

36. Abul Fazal Huq, "Bangladesh : Constitution, Politics and Bureaucracy," The Rajshahi University Studies, Part-A, Vol. XI, 1980-83, p. 34.

Under zia the state principle of socialism was re placed by economic and social justice, such an approach could produce better economic resulsts and a greater quantity of social gains could be made. But it no way guaranteed that exploitation of the poor would automatically disappear.

Table-5

Zia's Last Council of Ministers, 1981[37]
(Among 24 Full Minister in the Cabinet)

Professional Background	Number
Military Bureaucrats	6
Civil Bureaucrats	5
Technocrats	6
Businessmen	4
Landlord	1
Lawyer	2

Socialism, was, like capitalism not incompatible with corruption and social justice. Under the regime of zia the main issues of food, employment, population control were better understood, Zia made efforts for "curbing the growth rate of population, providing more job opportunities, social and economic developments and building up of a self-

37. Statistical year book of Bangladesh. (Dhaka : Bureau of Statistics, Government of Peoples Republic of Bangladesh, 1981), p.8.

reliant economy"[38] President Zia's approach was probably the only possible approach in the socio-political and economic framework of the country. The reaction against urban bias and the importance given to rural development were extremely sensible developments, no matter what the ideology. Zia also tried to reorganised the military which came in politics only to aid the civil affairs. President Zia-ur-Rahman tried to bring certain stability to his country by wiping out all differences between different factions of armed forces and established complete and unquestioned command. Zia turned himself from a military rule to a civilian by forming his own political party (B.N.P.). But, always pre-occupied with the maintenance and strengthening of his own position zia had not been able to direct any well considered policy for the removal of the economic agony of the people.

General zia was known for his personal honesty, but corruption of all sorts became rampant during his regime. A report wrote, "corruption has been converted from a crime to a habit and the acknowledgement of this fact has led to a faster growth of corruption in the country. Following it has appeared political corruption which has taken upon itself the protection of other crimes."[39] Military personnel appointed at civil posts drew all the concessions from the government. Practically the attempt was made to solve the basic problem of generating resources for development while maintaining the minumum consumption levels. Policies were ill-concevied and further

---

38. For detail see Bangladesh Times April 4, 1979. pp. 5, 6.

39. Quoted in V.P. Puchkov, Op. cit. p. 133.

impounded by inefficiency and corruption. Unemployment in Bangladesh was rising. There was no great effort to spread literacy among the masses. Primary education was as neglected as ever. Poverty of the masses, like their diseases, was endemic. While the large majority of people were rapidly sliding the poverty line, a handful of the rich continued to be more and more prosperous. 51% of all peasant families in Bangladesh in 1979 did not own any land, while in 1964 landless families had accounted for 29%.[40] Thus, the economic distress and exploitation of poor posed a challenge to the zia administration. "The Policy outputs of zia's government were not indicative of being able to create social inputs, which could provide a basic support for his leadership. There was no evidence of the existence of feedback loop."[41]

Unimproved social and economic tasks contributed to the agony of people. Zia's attempt to completely civilianise his rule through democratic traditions and to offer highly professionalised role to the army caused concern among the ambitious army personnel, who negated the move.

The deteriorating political situation combined with socio-economic crisis resulted in the killing of Zia-ur-Rahman, by a group of twenty officers at Chittagong. Apart from political vacuum, deteriorating socio-economic situtation, the faction ridden politicised army contributed a lot for this coup.[42] After the assassination of Zia-ur-

40. Ibid. p. 132.

41. S.K. Chakravarty, "The Evolution of Politics in Bangladesh : 1947-78" (New Delhi : Associated Publishing House, 1978), p. 256.

Rahman. President abdus Sattar, ensured a relatively smooth succession and then was elected President, comfortably defeating his chief challenger Dr. Kamal Hossain of Awami League. Within weeks the unease of armed forces with the apparent indecisiveness and continuing factionalism among leading politicians, led to General Ershad's coup, reimposing military rule and martial law in early 1982. gen. Ershad opted for greater role of military in the sphere of politics, in order to enhance the process of nation-building and improve other socio-economic problems faced by the poor country like Bangladesh. Ershad emphasised on bringing political stability by tackling the issues effectively. On the role of military he expressed, "Our military is an efficient, well disciplined most honest body of truly dedicated and organised national force. Potentials of such an excellent force in a poor country like ours can be effectively utilised for productive and nation building purposes in addition to its role in national defence."[43]

"In the middle of 1982 Ershad announced the introduction of 'new industrial policy' in the country, in accordance with preference was shown to the private sector and the role of the state sector was diminished at the same time. Only six branches of industry were allowed to remain with the state sector; the production of armaments and military equipment, atomic energy, air transport, telecommunications, electrical power and timber exploitation."[44]

---

42. For details see : Chapter-military Establishment.
43. For detail see Ershad's speech.
44. V.P. Puchkov, Op. cit. p. 182.

The new industrial policy provided not only for extensive measures to encourage the private sector-including a sharp increase in the volume of government resources to stimulate it but also the denationalisation of the basic branches of the economy.

During Ershad's administration the economic liberalism expanded. Steps were taken to denationalising industry and even banking and government tried to provide more acceptable climate for foreign investors. However, Bangladesh could not attract any significant level of foreign investment due to endemically unstable political situation.

In order to establish his command, Ershad appointed military personnel at various civilian posts. He, through the military power tried to monopolise his dictatorial rule and destroyed all the democratic tendencies which had started faning strength at the hands of Zia's policies. Ershad established his full sutocracy. The military continued to draw the concessions and previleges from the government. The economy continued to deteriorate. The social conditions became worse.

In March 1983, Ershad announced a programme of action of his administration in the socio-economic field, called the '18-point programme'. The programme was very much similar to the charater of '19-point programme' announced by Zia-ur-Rahman, in 1977. "The programme retained the goal of priority development of agriculture, the achievement of self sufficiency by the country in food stuffs, struggle against corruption etc.[45] Trying to find a

45. Bangladesh Observer, March 18, 1983, p. 4.

support among the masses Ershad introduces a number of populist slogans like "equal distribution of national wealth," "bridging the gap between the rich and the poor" and "carrying out agrarian reforms which would give justice to the life of the peasantry."[46]

The efforts of the military administration to solve socio-economic problems through the creation of favourable conditions for the development of the country along with capitalist path did not bring about any noticeable results. According to the data provided by the bank of Bangladesh, the G.N.P. grew in real terms by 8.7% in 1982-83 instead of the planned target of 6%. Industry continued to remain in a stagnant state and its growth during the year 1982-83 constituted only 0.4%. The share of industrial production in the G.N.P. decreased to 8.33%.[47]

The economic situation in 1984-85 was extremely difficult. The growth of economy as a whole was of the order of 4.2% in 1983-84 and 3.8% in 1984-85.[48] The state of economy was further aggravated by natural calamities, sich as floods and hurricanes.

Bangladesh heavily depended on imports. Share of her imports to G.D.P. was about 14% on average over a period of 15 years from 1972 to 1986. The lowest being 8.6% in 1974 during Mujib regime and the highest being 18.4% in

---

46. Ibid.

47. Bangladesh Times, Dec. 14, 1983, p. 2.

48. Bangladesh Observer, July 1, 1985, p. 3.

1986 during the military regime of Ershad.[49] The deficit in foreign trade remained quite considerable. Income from exports consituted about 900 million dollars, expenditure on imports 2700 million dollars.[50]

In 1983, Bangladesh's imports totalled approximately $ 1.5 billion and its exports totalled about $0.8 billion, leaving a deficit of $713 million. In fact, the export earning dropped below an annual rate of $ 500 million in 1985.[51] In 1989-90 the foreign trade showed exports of Taka 50.1 billion and imports of Tk 104.9 billion.[52] The total imports and exports during two military regimes show that exports remained always less than the imports, always resulting in increasing the balance of trade. The average balance of trade which during Zia regime was about 1203 million dollars (current) increased to about 1730 million dollars (current).[53] This increasing balance of trade had adverse effect on the socio-economic condiitions of Bangladesh.

---

49. Quoted in Prakash Chand Adhikarey & M. Sirazzuddin Biswas : "Potential Gains to Bangladesh from Imports of Selected commodities from India and Pakistan : An Analytical Investigation," India Quarterly, Vol. XLVII, No. 4, Oct.-Dec. 1991, p. 63.

50. V.P. Puchkov, Op. cit. p. 186.

51. Bangladesh Observer, Oct. p. 1985, p. 5.

52. Statistical Year Book of Bangladesh, Op. cit, 1990. p. 6.

53. Calculated from the Tables : 6 & 7.

Table-6

Total Imports and Exports During zia Regime :[54]

Year	Total Imports million dollars (current)	Total Exports million dollars (current)
1976	952	401
1977	1163	476
1978	1513	548
1979	1908	659
1980	2599	758
1981	2699	791

Table-7

Total Imports and Exports under Ershad's Regime :[55]

Year	Total Imports million dollars (current)	Total Exports million dollars (current)
1982	2463	769
1983	2165	724
1984	2825	931
1985	2772	999
1986	2702	880
1987	2987	1231

54. World Military Expenditure and Arms Transfers, (Washington : D.C. 1986), p. 92.

55. Ibid.

The problems facing the economy of Bangladesh became deep and serious during the military regime of Ershad. Bangladesh continued to receive finacial aids from abroad. The financial aid sice 1971 to 1984 reached the total amount of 16,425 million dollers.[56] In both the regimes i.e. Zia and Ershad, in first two years of their rule there was decline in the imports but in successive years imports were tremendously increased. Thus, militry regimes were more prone to extenrnal pressures. They prove to be inefficient in making the country self-sufficient.

The growth of foreign indebtness of Bangladesh kept on increasing. This laid a heavy burden on the economy of the country. With every passing year, Bangladesh had to pay to its western creditors larger and larger amounts to pay off the debts and the interest on them. "If during the decade 1972-81 the country had to pay 454 million dollars (273 million dollars of the loan and 181 million dollars ad interest) in 1981-82 it had to pay not less than 117.4 million dollars, in 1982-83, 136 million dollars and in 1984-85 the amount of repayments jumped to 350 million dollars."[57]

According to official figures Bangladesh had to pay 410 million dollars in 1985-86 and 480 million dollars in 1986-87 which constituted 24.3% and 28% respectively of the export earning of the country.[58] The life expactancy of any regime in Bangladesh thus, has been in the hands of the leaders of developed capitalist countries. The economic conditions became even worse under Ershad's regime. He could not improve the overall economy of the

---

56. V.P. Puckhov. Op. cit. p. 179.
57. Ibid, p. 181.

country. Economic liberalisation policies helped only the dominating classes as they got favours from the government. The socio-economic status of weak classes could not improve, which caused for despair and frustration among masses and for propelling a change in political leadership.

Under Ershad's regime corruption remained rampant as befors. The studies of BIDS (Bangladesh Insitute of Development Studies) reveal that 50% to 90% of all transactions in the financial sector were carried out outside the regular framework, the value of the black market in financial services amounted to 20% of official GDP, and the concerned firms were few and owned by families related to the ruling elite. Also, 50% of the identity business was in the hands of the 2% of the total number of firms working as commission agents for the aid funded projects."[59]

"The aggravated socio-economic problems increased the crime rate. The police registered 60,323 crimes in 1984 (as against 57,809 in 1983) including 1,993 murders. Smuggling of contraband goods assumed exteremely alarming pro-protions. According to the most modest estimates the cost of contraband goods which crossed the borders of Bangladesh was valued at 4 million Taka."[60]

The social conditions reamained acute during Ershad's regime. Natural calamilites further accelerated unemploy

---

58. Ibid.

59. Shyamali Ghosh, "Bangladesh Again at Cross Roads," Mainstream, Vol. XXIX, No. 9, Saturday, Dec. 22, 1990, p. 6.

60. V.P. Puckhov, Op.cit, p. 186.

ment and cost of living. "According to official figures, there were eleven million unemployed persons in the country in 1982-83. The cost of living in Dhaka between 1982-85 rose by 13-14% annually. The daily food ration of Bangladesh was reduced during the last two decades from 2300 calories to 1900 calories, 60% of the families in rural areas of the country received only upto 1500 calories per day."[61] "The World Bank Experts in 1984 reported that 86% of the population of Bangladesh lived below the official poverty line. "There was a very little growth in the production of foodstuffs which increased during 1976-83 by an average of 3.1%. In spite of the steps taken in the field of education, the percentage of the illiterates increased in the population. 76% of the children up to 15 years of age (and in 1984 these constituted 46.6% of the population) could not read or write."[62]

The extreme deterioration of socio-economic conditions of the country under the autocratic regime, hightened the aspirations of the masses for the democratic rule. Such aspirations led the masses to fight against the autocratic government.

During Ershad regime only a section of social strata gained ground, and that was the military, He relied heavily on military, the professional background of his council of ministers in July 1982 was as below:[63]

---

61. Ibid.
62. Ibid.

63. Abul Fazal Huq, "Bangladesh : Constitution, Politics and Bureaucracy," Rajshahi University Studies, Part-A Vol. XI, 1980-83, p. 34.

Table-8

Professional Background	Number
Military Bureaucrats	7
Civil Bureaucrats	3
Technocrats	2
Lawyer	4

The Main cause of the 1990 upsurge was that even under the military regimes Bangladesh remained "still in the early stages of political development, it had severe limitations in economic development and was restricted in social development by the instablity of political system and this weakened its economy."[64]

Ershad was moved out of power as the democratic forces combined to move into the political sphere. As a result, a democratically elected government came into force in 1991. It is headed by Begum Khalida Zia. Begum Begum Zia emphasised on the democratic norms. She said, "let us remain above all divisive tendencies, malices, wavering and conflict; and build a solid foundation of national cohesion by unitedly giving democracy a permanednt institutional shape."[65] "Democracy is the watch word in

64. Craig Baxter, "The Struggle for Development in Bangladesh," Current History, Vol. LXXIII, No. 378, Dec. 1989, p. 439.

65. The Bangladesh Times. March 26, 1992, p. 2.

politics now."[66] Emphasising on democratic traditions F. Karim wrote, "Fundamental of all fundamentals in that first of all one has to believe in the norms of democracy in one's very heart of hearts and then practice the same meticulously in ones own life both at home and abroad. Then and then alone one can devote oneself to pratice the same in the political sphere and in political administration."[67] Hence, the role of military in politics can decline only when every individual in the society gives importance to the democratic norms and believes in democratic values.

With the advent of civil regime under the leadership of Begum Zia. military has gone back to barracks and reins of bureaucracy have come in the hands of newly emerged class of politicians. These newly elected politicians are from Industrial and business class.

The prefessional background of the ministers of Khalida Zia's ministry (Table : 9) shows that the polity of Bangladesh has come into the hands of industrial-business class, which has no political experience. The success of regime would ultimately depend on improving the socio-economic conditions by building effective democratic institutions.

---

66. Dewan Md. Azraf in Bangladesh Observer, March 26, 1992, p. 4.

67. F. Karim in Bangladesh Observer, April 4, 1992, p. 1.

Table-9

Profession and Background of the Ministers of Khalida Zia's Ministery :[68]

Profession	Number
Lawyers	8
Businessmen & Industrialists	18
Former army officers now businessmen and Industrialists	5
Landholders	1
University and College Professors	5
Former Government officers	2
Full Time politicians	1

The new government has attempted to meet the requirements placed on it by the International monetary fund. One step in this direction was the introduction of a value added tax, which met with opposition, but as modified somewhat, has remained in the effect and should be more readily collectable than some other taxed. The economy remains very much in deficit both internally and externally. Budget estimates of receipts fall far short of expenditure requirements adn foreign assistance remains essential. The foreign debt burden was reduced to some extent when the United Staes forgave about $ 260 million indebts

68. Talukder Maniruzzaman. "The Fall of the military Dictator : 1991 Elections and the Prospect of Civilian Rule in Bangladesh," Pacific Affairs Vol. LXV, No. 2, Summer, 1992, p. 217.

that had long been on the books. Most current bilateral assistance from all donors is in the form of grants.[69] Efforts to increase foreign investment have generally been unsuccessful. The privatisation programme is continuing, but the climate for investment is hindered by continuing law and order problems, and also due to the shortage of natural and financial resources within Bangladesh. According to world Bank Report- 1992, the decline in the annual G.D.P. growth rate has been significant. At market prices, the G.D.P. stands at $ 22.5 billion with growth declining form a peak of 7.5% during five year plan 1975-80 (Zia's period) to 5.2% during five year plan-1981-86, to 4.0% during five year plan 1987-89, further declining to 3.6% in 1990-91.[70] If the decline is not arrested soon Bangladesh's dependence on external resources will become even more acute creating an increasingly tenable socio-economic situation.

Despite political uncertainties, Bangladesh economy has been growing. It grew at an estimated 6.7 % in 2006. Poverty has been reduced by 1.78% and overall balance of payments remained satisfactory with trade dificit decreasing to US$ 417 million in the first quarter of fiscal year, 2007, even if the inflation remains high at 6.9%.

---

69. Craig Baxter, "Bangladesh in 1991, A Parliamentary System," Asian Survey, Vol. XXXII, No. 2, Feb, 1992, pp. 166-167.

70. World Bank Report, 1992 (Washington : D.C. 1992) p. 10265.

(Source : Bangladesh : Quaterly Economic Update, Asian Development Bank, 2006 and 2007). The challenges in socio-economic modernization of Bangladesh remains to be tackled under political uncertainties, lack of economic expertise which could delineates political and ideological influences for economic progess for eg. supension of Tata deal with India by the BNP government. Such incidents present to the world the picture that Bangladesh may not be the most attractive place for industrial investment. Also, internally there was unrest in the garment industry over minimum wages.

There have been instances of threats to internal securities in the form of crime and political violence on one hand and terrorism and religious extermism on the other. "a heady cocktail of crime, terrorism and politics is the hallmark of Bangladesh to-day."[71]

However the reports of Bangladesh becoming safe heaven for terrorists have been dubbed by the Bangladesh government as, "inimical propaganda" to malign the international image of the country."[72] Recently, some steps have been taken to wipe out extermists from Bangladesh soil. The media, both Indian and Bangladesh have published the reports of terrorist training camps in the North-east

---

71. In an interview in New Delhi, Wasbir Hussain, Director, Centre for development and Peace Studies, Guwahati : on December 11, 2006.

72. Haroon Habin, "Electoral Warfare" Front line, November 3, 2006. p. 57.

and Southern regions of Bangladesh.[73]

The unperdictability of oil prices also undermines the socio-economic programme as it has long range implications on the price rise of all the commodities resulting due to transportation links.

Bangladesh is, still being faced with a series of contraditiions. There are contradictions between rural and urban development, and between agricultural and industrial development. There is also a contradition between rich and poor classes in the society. Some of these contraditions were generated by capitalist penetration and the old colonoal rule of the British imperialist power. But some are the direct out come of the development strategies and descriminate socio-economic policies pursued by the ruling elite of pakistan and others are the deliberate creation of the ruling civil-military oligarchy of Bangladesh.

Militarys significance in financial autonomy has been also been a part of Bangladeshi socioeconomic processes whether by direct military personnel involvements or by their retired officials. Wheatever may be the levels of intervention by military in any affairs, there is always a risk of military stepping into politics of the country.

The analysis of socio-economic conditions under different periods of the regimes shows that no governement, whether that was military or civilian could lead to political stability under severe socio-economic crisis. zia started the process of liberalization of economy

73. 48 Military camps in Bangladesh : Report, Indian Express, Jan 13, 2004, Raunaq Jahan, Falure of Military Government, The Daily Star, March, 14, 2006.

and shunned the role of state. But great thrust on liberalization of economy was given by Ershad. Like most of military regimes, Bangladesh military regimes definitely favoured the status quo. Any attempt to radicalize the socio-economic order was met with by the military officers by force. Under the conditions of frustration the masses of Bangladesh opted for frequent changes in the government leadership and gave way to military in politics but when military also could not fulfil their expectations, they reverted back to democracy. Thus, the role which military played in the politics of Bangladesh was a test for it in which it failed. Hence, military can not be called as an agent of socio-economic modernization. In fact, military is instrument of socio-economic status-quo.

VI - Military Establishment

The prevaling environmental conditions of a country do not explain the phenomenon in its totality, until the nature of military establishement is taken into account. The environmental conditions are like catalytic agents, it is the nature of the military establishment which brings the componental changes in the society. The objective factiors are partial in themselves, if discussed without taking subjective factors.. Thus, the nature of military establishment includes all the factors, which pertain to the nature of military establishment, such as- size, structural composition, recruitment, ideologyl representativeness, level of cohesion and autonomy, hierarchial structure, level of professionalisation, corporate interests, social composition, as well as officerss class background, communal attitudes, training etc. of military establishment.

These variables provide for a significant guideline for the basic understanding of military's attitude and view point towards its playing an active role in political spheres of a country. Military establishment variables also explain the civil-military or politico-military relations and the potentials of military to come into the politics of any society as affected by environmental conditions.

Bangladesh had a legacy of dominating civil-military

elite first inherited from the Britishers and then from the Pakistan, These civil-military elites were all powerful and pervasive. They considered themselves to be the guardians of the v ast majority o f t he i lliterate and poverty stricken people. They had faith in the destiny of the country but had no faith in the ability of the people to govern themselves. As such these elite were apathetic to democratic path of development.

In fact, what Bangladesh got, was a highly politicised military. The process of politicisation of armed forced which had started in the colonial period continued under the second colonial period (Pakistan Period) also. The politicisation of military had three main factors[1] - first, the aid to civil phenomenon occured at regular intervals after 1949 in Pakistan whenever there were political crises, whether caused by communal riots as in 1950, 1952, 1954, 1963 and 1970, by a devastating flood, by periodic epidemics or by food shortage and near-famines, the army had always been called to help the civil administration. In these operations the armed personnel got themselves exposed to the prevailing political and economic corruptions and to the weaknesses of the politicians. Over time, these experiences contributed to the growth of groups within the armed forces and the ambitious armed officers with considerable daring and a little idealism, the differences of opinion on native issues, the policies and the modes of execution of the politices were the factors which led mili-

1. Zillur R. Khan, "Politicisation of the Bangladesh Military : A Response to Perceived Shortcomings of Civilian Government," Asian Survey, Vol. XXI, No. 5, May, 1981, pp. 551-52.

tary to intervene in the politics. But, in the case of Bangladesh millitary itself remained divided on various issues and policies, resulting in coups. Thirdly, the deterioration of economic conditions under the incompetent politicans led to the increased politicisation of armed forces.

In one critical respect however, the inheritence of armed forces of Bangladesh was very different from that of Pakistan. Bangladesh did not have a united armed force. The original army was formed with the East Pakistan Rifles and the Mukti Bahini, the freedom fighters from independence war, who were under the nominal control of Awami league. About 28,000 Bengali soldiers repatriated from Pakistan were also added to this strength.[2] "The Mukti Bahini component were mainly young, not well trained or disciplined, but highly politicised and publicly idolised as heroes of the freedom war. The Pakistan returnees were professionals, with longer training and service. Most of these offices and men shared the standards and values of Pakistan army. Most of their formative period had been under the Ayub-Yahaya martial law regimes and the military personnel played an important role in the rise of Bengali subnationalism during Pakistan era, they voiced concern about the neglect of Bengali rights and interests. And these elites participated in Bangladesh liberation war. In fact, they became champions of emerging nationalism

---

2. Gowher Rizvi, "Riding the Tiger : Institutionalising the military Regimes in Pakistan and Bangladesh" in Christopher Clapman and George Philip (eds.) The Political Dilemmas of Political Regimes, (London : Croom Helm Ltd. 1985), p. 224.

and undertook political role in deciding the future fate of the Bengalis in the later phase of the Pakistani period. The junior Bengali officers in the pakistani army were undoubtedly a well disciplined group, they also had become conscious of the Bengalis rights and aspirations. So the Bengali personnel of Pakistan armed forces played a heroic and important role during Banbladesh liberation movement. The result was that the Bengali personnel of the armed forces had an active experience in politics and political movements. The process of politicisation of the Bangladesh army and civil servants became complete with their involvenment in the liberation war of 1971. So, the highly politicised factions of the army of Bangladesh seemed to harbour an ambition of having some share in the political affairs of the country.

After liberation, the leadership of army remained in the hands of junior ranking officials, who had demonstated their organising ability and fighting qualities. The men recruited during the war came from different age groups and social backgrounds with different levels of education. They had no baisc or uniform training and did not undergo discipline similar to that of a regular army.. It is apparent that the young officers who fought in the liberation war with courage, success and sacrifice constituted the military elite in Bangladesh.

Although Bangladesh armed forces were ethinically, linguistically and religiously homogenous, factionalism erupted on personal and political lines. "The armed forces of Bangladesh were first a small mixture of Mukti Bahini fighters and fresh regular voluneers, to which in 1974 were

---

3. Ibid.

added the 28000 internal Bengali officers and soldiers who had sat out the December, 1971 war n West Pakistan internment camps, demanding to be reabsorved with priority in seniority, promotion and appointments. Thus began the internal struggle between the freedom fighters and the repatriates."[4] Hence, the bases of coups and counter-coups can be analysed in terms of loyalism of soldiers towards liberation war, which later, resulted in antagonistic attitudes towards repatriated soldiers.

The Mukti Bahini, which provided the bulk of recruits to different wings of the armed forces of independent Bangladesh consisted of deserters, soldiers and policemen, young and raw recruits. While the deserters represented a peasant based professional cadre; the young recruits, constituted 60% of the freedom fighters who were students from lower middle class who took up the sword instead of the pen for the sake of their country's freedom. A section of this youth was a votary of the Awami League ideology. But a big majority of them was left-oriented believing in the dictum "power comes from the barrel of the gun."[5]

The armed forces of Bangladesh constitute less than 0.08 percent of the country's population,[6] but occupy the most prominent place in the short but momentous history

---

4. Colonel Edgar O' Ballance, "Bangladesh : Orphan of the Storm," Armed Forces, Vol. VI No. 2, Feb, 1987, p. 62.

5. Indian Express, July 16, 1971.

6. Veena Kukreja, Civil-Military Relations in South Asia : Pakistan- Bengladesh and India. (New Delhi : Sage Publications, 1991). p. 131.

of the infant Republic. Defence structure is headed by president, manpower is provided by voluntary enlistment. Bangladesh ranks 14th in the world in per capita military strength.[7]

In an official press note of 26 December, 1971, the government of Bangladesh outlined important proposals aimed at raising a regular army, navy and airforce, and a national police force and military for internal security. The press note said the valiant Mukti Bahini provided a rich reservoir for the proposed security forces. Selection boards would be formed for the purpose of recruiting commissioned and non-commissioned officers. The government press note also said that a national defence academy would be set jup shortly to train new officer grades and other's for the nations defence forces.[8]

After the resignation of Gen. M.A.G. Osmany, former Gommander-in-Chief of Bangladesh armed forces on 7th April, 1972; the Bangladesh government abolished the combined command of the Bangladesh forces and created three separate service head-quarters, each under a chief of staff.[9]

About 28000 Bengali military personnel repatriated from Pakistan after April 1973,[10] freedom fighters and

---

7. Encylopaedia of Third World, Vol I (London : Mansell Publishing Ltd. 1992), p. 137.

8. P.B. Sinha, "Armed Forces of Bangladesh," IDSA Papers, Armed, Sept. 1979, occational Paper No. 1, p. 2.

9. Times of India, April 9, 1972.

10. The Times London, Jan. 14, 1972.

fresh recruits formed the armed-military and para-military / auxiliary forces of Bangladesh.

(a) Military force :

(i) Army : Army constituted the strongest and the most important wing of the armed forces in Bangladesh. Col K.M. Shafiullah was made first chief of army staff.[11] Col. Khalid Musharraf was made chief of the General staff.[12]

(ii) Navy : The forgmen in the Mukti Bahini, who sank Pakistani ships in Khulana and Chittagong during the war of liberation were set to constitute the Naval wing of freedom fighters. With the capture of 5 motorboats from Pak troops some time in october 1971, the Bangladesh Navy was formed as the nucleus of the future navy.[13] Connander Nurul Huq was made Chief of Naval Staff since April 7, 1972 when the three separate service commands were created.[14] After his repatriation from Pakistan, Captain Mosharaff Hossain Khan was promoted as Commodore and appointed on adhoc basis to act as Chief of Naval Staff November 6, 1973.[15]

In Bangladesh's military, navy plays an important role, as Bangladesh is a riverine country and has a vast coastline. "Bangladesh Navy, guards national coastline; harbours

11. The Hindu (Madras), April 9, 1972.
12. Bangladesh Observer, (Dhaka), Oct. 10, 1972.
13. Hindustan Standard (Calcutta), Oct. 17, 1971.
14. Hindu (Madras), April 9, 1972.
15. Hindustan Times (New Delhi), Feb. 26, 1976.

and off shore islands against seaward attacks, ensure free and uninterrupted flow of trade across the ocean, asists army and air force in amphibious operations, guards territorial waters, assists merchant navy in peace and war and provides assistance to civil-population in natural calamities like cyclones and floods.[16]

(iii) Air Force : Bangladesh Air Force (B.A.F.) : "budded and took roots on the firm grounds of reality."[17], with a few armed helicopters and other light air craft on 28 septmeber, 1971 as the air wing of the liberation forces. It was on 3 december, 1971 that the B.A.F. commenced its first aerial attack on Pakistani troops. After liberation, B.A.F. was found to have "inherited from the enemy nothing but shambles, destroyed air craft, damaged runway, looted stores, neutralised maintenance facilities-in short a disorganised mess."[18] But by September, 1973, the Chief of air staff was confident enough to declare that the B.A.F. "is now in a position, with regard to both men and equipment, to defend the air space of independent and soverign Bangladesh, to defend the air space of independent and soverign Bangladesh in the event of any foreign aggression on this country" as it was in a position "to detect, locate and identify any approaching air craft violating our air space with the help of radar and could launch counter

---

16. Bangladesh Observer, December 10, 1976.

17. Late Air-vice Marshal M.K. Bashar, "Birth of Bangladesh Air Force," Reproduced in Bangladesh Observer, September 9, 1977, p. 4.

18. Ibid.

attack with a half a mile of its entry inside the border."[19] In 1973 it was planned to activate Air force bases at Jessore and Chittagong in addition to the one already existing in Dacca.[20] Air commodore A.K. Khondker was made Chief of Air Stff on 7 April, 1972.[21]

(b) Para-Military / Auxiliary Forces :

(i) Bangladesh Rifles : After liberation the East Pakistan Rifles were reorganised and named as the Bangladesh Rifles (BDR).

(ii) Jatiyo Rakhi Bahini : Jatiyo Rakhi Bahini (J.R.B.), a militant armed force, was raised as a civil defence league after liberation. The most controversial of all the military and paramilitary forces, the J.R.B. was as much an object of speculation for foreign observers as it was target of criticism by anti-Mujib and anti-Awami League opposition elements. Officially its role was described as to help the police whenever necessary. In January 1974, a law was passed giving the Bahini protection against any legal action brought against it, allowing it the right of arrest without warrant and powers to search houses and property.[22]

The J.R.B. was created by Mujib as a personal security force, compared mainly of what have been described as "thugs and gangsters" in order to serve as a warning to the army, not to entertain any thoughts of mutiny."[23] The

---

19. Bangladesh Observer, Sept, 17, 1973.
20. Late Air Vice Marshal M.K. Bashar, op.cit.
21. Bangladesh Observer, Sept. 24, 1973.

22. Times of India, January 30, 1974.
23. Amit Roy, "Fall of an Idol," The Sun, August 21, 1975.

Western press called it "a couterpoise to the army,"[24] thus, it was a presidential guard, a secret police and an alternate army wrapped into one.

The strength of J.R.B., whose headquarters were located at Saver had been variously estimated between 10000 and 40000 during Mujib regime.[25]

(iii) Police : Like regular soldiers policemen too, in their thousands joined liberation force. After liberation Mujib announced for the formation of a new police force drawn from the Gram Bahini.[26] The reorganisation plan, which including the raising of its strength ultimately from 27,000 to 1000,000 involved an expenditure of Rs. 400 million.[27] Later more recruits were added. The first and foremost task of police force was to deal with continuing serious law and order situation in the country.

In order to streamline and modernise these forces, the government raised a Special Armed Force (SAF) as a component of the police force, to cambat the growing lawlessness in the country, the governemtn imported a large number of landrovers, jeeps, trucks and wireless sets to properly equip the new force. The number of out posts was increased from 310 to 500 and many damaged ones were renovated and replenished by men and material.[28]

(iv) Ansaras : The Ansar Organisation established on

---

24. Dilip Mukherjee, "Bangladesh Without Mujib : Problems Facing the New Regimes," Times of India, August 23, 1975.

25. Times of India, September 15, 1973.

26. Hindu Jan. 1, 1972.

27. Statesmen, March 2, 1972.

28. Bangladesh Observer, November 5, 1973.

12 February, 1948 was till 1976 a solely an irregualr auxiliary force. People, after giving training of six months were taken as Ansars. There was however, no regular structure for Ansars.[29]

The size of armed forces during Mujib Regime was as givin in Table : 1. Defence Expenditure in 1973-74 was Tk 470 million ($ US 65 million)[30]

Table-1

Armed Forces During Mujib Regime :[31]

Year	Total Regular Forces	Army	Navy	Airforce	Paramilitary forces
1975	26,500	25,000	500	1,000	16,000 National Defence Force, 1300 Bangladesh Rifles

Mujib came to power with profound distrust of the civil-military elite under which he had suffered during ayub and Yahaya regimes. The ruling elite during Mujib regime were the awami league members, who mainly came from landlord classes. Unsure of the ideological commitments of different sections of the Bangladesh liberation forces,

29. Bangladesh Observer, October 29, 1977.
30. The Military Balance, (London : 1974-1975), p. 52.
31. Ibid, pp. 52-53.

Mujib sought to raise a division of security forces which would have unquestioned loyality to the new regime, called the Jatio Rakhi Bahini (National Security Army), this new contingent was designed as a counter-vailing force to the Bengladesh regular army. The creation of privileged Rakhi Bahini was resented by the army, which feared that it might one day be used against itself. Thus, the differences got aggravated and generated serious conflicts between the command structure of two parallel armies. "Revolutionary changes took place within the Bengali army with various groups aligning themselves with sundry political parties and ideologies. Political considerations became foremost in shaping their political outlook, they felt that their contribution to the liberation war was of such magnitude that they were entitled to a share in a political power."[32] So, the political apparatus that Mujib had, was defective in itself. Most of the people in Awami league and Mukti Bahini were from various different sections and had different ideologies. The faulty organization of military structure proved to be fatal for democratic experience.

These different factions did not co-people with each other and indulged in selfish motives. Most of the people who had acquired weapons during liberation periods did not return them and indulged in strengthening their own positions after independence, Such Bengali guerillas, who substantially came from rural areas used power through the automatic weapons. During 1972 the government,

32. Dilara Choudhury, "Challenges to Democracy in Bangladesh." Regional Studies, Vol. V. No. 1, Winter, 1986-87. p. 30.

through a mixed policy of appeals, threats and rewards collected considerable amounts of arms and ammunition from freedom fighters, but huge amounts of arms and ammunition had not been surrendered hence, the armed robberies and attacks on police posts through automatic weapons continued.

"Mujib called for the surrender of arms by the Mukti Bahini and the various guerilla units within ten-days time limit and reitereated his earlier belief that power doed not come from the barrel of the gun but rather stems from the people."[33]

There were a number of secret killings, "one government estimate put the figure over 6000 persons killed, mostly for political reasons."[34] The political conditions became worse under Mujib regime. There were factions in Awami league and Mukti Bahini. Thus, he failed to provide for an umbrella organisation. In order to control the situation, he applied autocratic policies which further deteriorated the conditions.

Stating about the military, Mujib, in the Jatiya Sangsad reiterated, "I want my army a people's army. I do not want my army to fight against anybody. But I want my army to defend myself and at the same time to work."[35] Thus western nation of professionalism of military was discarded

---

33. The Bangladesh Observer, (Dacca), Jan. 19, 1972.

34. A.T.R. Rahman, "Administration and its Political Environment in Bangladesh" in Pacific Affairs Vol. XLVII 1974, p. 182.

35. Quote in M. Nazrul Islam, "Crisis of Politics in Bangladesh," South Asian Studies, Vol. XXIV, No. 2, July-Dec., 1989, p. 90.

by Mujib in the beginning only. This paved the way for the politicisation of Bangladesh military.

The regime allocated a lion's share of army expenditure to Jatiya Rakhi Bahini (JRB), the politically motivated paramilitary force. While the allocation for defence increaced by about 87.5% from Tk. 40 crores in 1972-73 to Tk. 75 crores in 1975-76 budget. The allocation for J.R.B. during the same period increased by about 190% from Tk 7.70 crocres to Tk. 22.69 crores.[36] This disproportionate allocation of funds developed friction between J.R.B. and regular armed forces.

The government planned to increase the strength of J.R.B. from about 28000 in 1975 to 130000 in 1980, while recruitment to the regular armed forces was virtually stopped in 1975.[37] The anti-Indian sentiment of armed forces developed into anti-Mujib orientation. Military gradually became antagonised towards the ruling elite, who used the army to correct their own failures and at the same time damaged the military's image by calling off the operations before they were completed. Military became aware of the corrupt practices, weaknesses and failures the Awami league politicians.

The Awami league could not evolve a rational policy towards the armed forces. The freedom fighters became

---

36. Ibid.

37. Talukdar Maniruzzaman, "Bangladesh in 1975 : The Fall of the Mujib Regime and its Aftermath," Asian Survey, Vol. XVI Feb. 1976, p. 122.

frustrated by the lack of concern the government displayed for their rehabilitation. On the other hand, J.R.B. was being used as an armed cadre of ruling party and received preferential treatment from the government. The situation gave rise to dissatisfaction among the military elite.

The Mukti Bahini and Awami league worked together as military and civilian army in the freedom struggle. While the Awami league Mukti Bahini was run largely by moderate democratic nationalists who demanded little social change in Bangladesh, the leftist freedom fighting youth generally believed that independence was just one, though essential step on the path of socio-economic emancipation of the masses.

Hence, later on the ideological differences cropped up in the armed forces. The armed forces of Bangladesh developed several verticle divisions on ideological grounds. These could be placed under three broad groups.[38] The first group was of rightists, reactionaries and communalists. Thous, forced by circumstances they formed part of the armed forces of an independent, secular state, the members of this group forces of an independent, secular state, the members of this group were not prepared to accept the changes. Air Vice Marshal Tawab and like minded members of the armed forces could be put in this category. The second group could be called as 'Mujibist', believing in the four state principles of nationalism, secularism, socialism and democracy and owning

---

38. P.B. Sinha, "Armed Forces of Bangladesh," IDSA Papers, Armed, Sept, 1979, Occasional Paper No. 1, pp. 29-30.

personal loyality to sheikh Mujib. The Jatio Rakhi Bahini exclusively and many members of other wings of armed forces could be said to belong to this group. The Left oriented members of the armed forces, owing allegiance to various extremist socialist political parties and leaders, could be clubbed in the third group. From the point of view of degree of influence exercised among the members of the armed forces, and significance in the part played in developments connected with the armed forces, and significance in the part played in developments connected with the armed forces of Bangladesh, the Jatiyo Samaj-Tantric dal occupied the most Leftist parties. Abu Taher and his group can be categorised in this group, who forwarded 12-point demand charter to Zia-ur-Rahman.

Some of the Army officers such as Major M. Jalil, Lt. Col. M. Ziauddin and Col. Abu Taher were dismissed from the armed forces due to ideological differences.[39] Apart from ideological divisions, the armed forces of Bangladesh have been suffering from rivalries, jealousies, mutual antagonisms, groupism and factionalism, whether between different wings of the forces or within one wing itself. The groups were based not only on ideological basis but also had intense personal rivalries, Mujib, thus, "built up the chain of command in the army like a delicately balanced house of cards."[40] As long as the towering personality of the Sheikh was there, the mutual rivalries and feuds in the armed forces could not raise their

39. For Detail see Ibid.

40. Daniel Burger, "Sheikh's Legacy of Confusion," Far Eastern Economic Review, Sept. 5, 1975, p. 16.

head. His liquidation led to the collapse of the house of cards.

The armed forces of Bangladesh were thus, highly factionalised, discontented and dissatisfied with their position. They were highly politicised due to their role in liberation struggle and played role as 'aid to civil' after liberation. They felt humiliated also due to their suspension of operations. The forces lacked in equipment and training. The armed forces of Bangladesh were thus, less professionalised. All these factors led the armed forces of Bangladesh to play an active role in the politics of the country.

Army stepped into the politics of the country after a series of coups. First was the coup of 15 August, 1975 in which Mujib along with his family members was killed. The coup was plotted by about 47 army officers of the ranks of Major, Captain and Lieutenant. The leadership of the group was concentrated in the hands of six majors. Dalim, Adbur Nur, Farooq Rahman (Bengal Lancers armed Regiment) Khondkar Adbur Rashid, (2nd Field Artillery Regiment), a nephew of the new president, Abdul Hafiz and M. Huda.[42] The coup was carried out by young offiers, who had personal vengeance against Mujib and wanted to liquidate the Sheikh dynasty and topple his government. The young officers had conflicts with awami league politicians, and some of them had been cashiered from the army on this basis. These officers had, thus no intention

41. P.B. Sinha, Op.cit. p. 15.

42. Lawrence Lifschult, "The Army's Blueprint for a Takeover," Far Eastern Economic Review, Sept. 5, 1976. p. 9.

to play a political role neither they were capable of playing a political role. After the coup, Khondkar Mushtaq Ahmed, a conservative and relatively anti-Indian and pro-American was installed as President. The coup makers had no future plans. They did not have full command of the army and could not displace senior army officers who were not directly involved in the coup and most of whom were pro-Mujibist. They army, thus, got divided into two camps-Pro-Mujibist and anti-Mujibist elements. Hence, the struggle for power thus, started between coup makers and senior officers, which resulted in a second coup of November 3, 1975, i.e. twelve weeks after the first coup.

The second coup was led by Brigadier Khaled Mushrraf the army second-in command. He was pro-Indian and pro-Mujibist. Several senior officers Seized power. These were the amibitios officers, who wanted to salvage Mujibism, but who did not realise that majority of the Bengali elite were still haunted by bitter memories of the later Mujib regime. Musharaff was widely regarded as India's man and this aroused intense opposition within the army. Sensing the anti-coup and Mujib revival sentiments, a radical group within the army. Sensing the anti-coup and anti-Mujib revival sentiments, a radical group within the army belonging to the Jatiyo Samajtantrik Dal (J.S.D.) which was formed by a number of dissidents and Marxists within the Awami league party in 1972, who had been organising within army, emerged on the scene. J.S.D. and Abu Taher organised Peoples Revolutionary Army. They distributed a number of leaflets within the army and presented twelve demands charter. (See Appendix-VIII). As a result, the army got factionalised on ideological lines. The inspired soldiers under the leadership of Abu Taher, freed Zia, who had been arrested by Mussaraf. So Khalid's coups proved to be short lived and he was killed in the coup by soldiers uprising, which took the form of full-blooded revolution. By the evening of 7th November, 1975 things took a more organised shape. Maj. Gen. Zia-ur-Rahman was reinstalled as the Chief of Staff of the Bangladesh Army.[43] The series of coups was the result of factionalism within the army. The army had become highly politicised. "The primates who had been responsible for restoring Zia were highly politicised, had killed a large number of their own officers and were unlikely to return to barracks without extracting their pound of flesh."[44]

Although, in the pressure of the moment Zia had agreed to the demands presented by Abu Taher, they obviously were not consistent with the type of army he envisioned. In order to organise the extremely weak army, many J.S.D. leaders were later killed and arrested by Zia. Taher was sentensed to death. Rab and Jalil got life imprisonment.

The military as it came to power in 1975 after coups and counter coups presents that highly factionalised armed forces lacked discipline. Zia continued to face various oppositions against him. It is reported that there occured as many as 27 attempted coups to overthrow him.[45]

---

43. Veena Kukreja, Op. cit, p. 145.

44. Gowher Rizvi, Op. cit. pp. 225-226.

45. Azizul Haque, "Bangladesh in 1980 : Strains and Stresses-Opposition in Doldrums", Asian Survey Vol. XXI, No. 2, Feb. 1981, p. 582.

In the wake of the August 1975 putsch a major reshuffle took place in the top army command. Gen. (retd.) M.A.G. Osmany was made the President's Defence Advisor. Maj. Gen. Zia-ur-Rahman was made Chief of Army Staff. Brig. H.M. Ershad was promoted to the rank of Maj. Gen. and made Deputy Chief of Army Staff.[46] The repatriates were now placed in most key positions in armed forces.

M.H. Khan continued to be the Chief of Naval Staff. There were three Naval establishments in Bangladesh-Chittagong, Khulana and Dacca. The newly constructed Bangladesh naval Headquarters was inaugurated in January[47] 1977. It was then disclosed that a training institute for the navy personnel would soon be established.[47] In July 1977 the government of Bangladesh decided to establish a defence services command and staff college in Dacca soon, with the assistance of the British Government. Col. Muzammel Hussain of Bangladesh Army was designated as its first commandent.

Due to the differences with Zia, Air Vice Marshal M.G. Tawab resigned and his place was taken over by Air Gommodore M. Khademul Bashar, he was made Chief of the staff[49] of B.A.F. the abortive coup of 2 October, 1977 in Dacca inflicted a heavy blow on the B.A.F. Eleven officers of Air force-two group captains, one wing commander, one squardon leader, two flight Lieutenants, two

46. Patriot, Nov. 22, 1975.

47. Ibid

48. Bangladesh Observer, July 21, 1977.

49. Hindustan Times, May 4, 1976.

Flying officer and three Pilot officers were killed during the attempted coup.[50]

Bangladesh rifles were transformed by Zia as a better, bigger and stronger force. They were modernised in terms of weapons, equipment and communication facilities. He announced that, "plans to expand and modernise B.D.R. further were in the process of formulation and implementaion."[51] "Maj. Gen. M. Khillur Rahman, Director General of B.D.R. was made chief of Defence Staff in the ministry of Defence and the Brigade Commander, Chittagong Brig. Qaazi Golam Dastagir was promoted as Maj, Gen and appointed Director Gen. of B.D.R."[52]

The J.R.B. was absorbed in the army by Zia. A new special police force, a sort of private army was raised by Zia after reorganising the police force. "The force was designed to combat crimes of a special nature, articularly where sophi-sticated weapons were involved. It was also to carry out special drives, mopping up operations and other activities requiring special traning and techniques. the battalions were to have no permanent base, but would always be in combat readiness to serve any where in the country."53 Zia gave preference to these forces just as Mujib had prefered J.R.B. Both the rulers gave rise to a sort of personal armies thereby politicising the military as such.

---

50. Bangladesh Observer, Oct, 4, 1977.

51. Bangladesh Observer April 1, 1977.

52. Hindustan Times Dec. 31, 1975.

53. Michael Chinoy, "Decca's Strongman Consolidates," Far Eastern Economic Review, Jan. 16, 1976, p. 24.

The Ansars Organisation was fundamentaly restructured in 1976. It was designated as 'people's defence force and 'second line of defence' of the country. By October, 1977, battalions of regular Ansars, numbering 6,000 had been raised. The total number of people enrolled as Ansars (including irregular) was about one million in October, 1977, From 1976 the Ansar Organisation started recruiting women.[54] The first batch of 600 prospective trained company commanders of Ansars came out of the Ansar Training Centre, Saver, in June 1976.[55]

Table-2

Armed Forces During Zia Regime:[56]

Year	Total Regular Forces	Army	Navy	Airforce	Paramilitary forces
1975	26,500	25,000	500	1,000	16,000 National Defence & 13000 B.D.R.
1980-81	72,000	65,000	4000	3000	3000 B.D.R.& 36000 Armed Police reserved

54. Bangladesh Obserever Oct. 29, 1977.
55. Ibid, June 30, 1976.
56. Military Balance, (London : 1974-75 and 1980-81)

Table-3

Defence Expenditure:[57]

Year	Tk.	$ M.
1975	470 m	65
1980	2.5 bn	153

Thus Zia distributed the national cake in favour of Army by increasing military exdpenditure.

In order to consolidated his position and to legitimise his rule, Zia promulgated new laws. Martial law superseded the constitution adopted in 1972. The National Economic Council was revived and made responsible Commission. The budget of 1976-77 allocated 29% of the total budget for defence and security forces.[58] Implementation of Planning remained firmly in the hands of civil servants, who like most of the senior military officers, were trained in the Pakistani tradition of martial law. To increase co-ordination of civil and military operations in the rural areas, district level Zonal Martial Law Administrators were appointed. The economy affected by Mujib in defence budgets was thron overboard and despite pressing claims for funds in other sectors, expenditure was lavishly increased, "Mujib's 1974-75 defence budget of 750 million

57. Ibid.

58. M. Choudhury, "Military Coups and Military Rule in Bangladesh," Indian Journal of Politics Vol, No. 34, June-Dec. 1983, p. 108.

takes was raised to 2063 million, from 13% to nearly 29% of total revenue budget."[59]

A new army division was raised to provide both a loyal force for Zia and promotions for the officers. Intelligence systems were geared up, a speical combat force of 12,500 men raised for counter insurgency duties, and the Bangladesh rifles, and adjunct of the army, raised from 40,000 to 70,000 men.[60]

Murders, roberies and riots were little reduced after Zia assumed power. But unreported murders, kidnapping for political and business reasons continued in the country side. A direct recapture of illegal arms was started which tightened.

During 1977 sporadic and seemingly unconnected and un-coordinated mutinies occured mong troops in different parts of Bangladesh, the more serious ones taking place in Chittagong within the naval base and in Rajshahi, Rangpur and Bogra. However, these uprisings followed a common pattern inevitably involving common soldiers who challenged the existing military hierarchy. These mutinies lacked leadership. But the uprisings revealed the hand of an ideological group, the same as or at least similar to Taher's that was testing the strength and will of the officer class and Zia's loyal followers within the Bangladesh armed forces. Such mutinies continued and then there was a coup in October against Zia. From the coup it was evident that the October 2, 1977 coup was a

---

59. Gowhar Rizvi, Op.cit, p. 226.
60. Ibid.

planned coup as can be drawn from the earlier uprisings, Also, it was not an isolated incident but the climax of all the efforts to establish a classless armed force.

The coup of 2nd October, 1977 was to topple the zia government. It was led by a group of non-commissioned air-force officers and airmen along with a group of non-commissioned army officers, junior commissioned officers and soldiers of Dhaka Cantonment.[61] These soldiers beleived in leftist ideology and wanted the abolition of British Colonial practices within the armed forces of Bangladesh. These soldiers adopted the Taher's ideological revolutionary socialist path. What irritated the Taherites was Zia's attitute to socialism, which got amended, out of existence when explained in terms of social justice and equity. Since Zia's assumption of power, not only the armed forces but also the economy and polity underwent a kind of change what they exactly wanted to circumvent.

Though unsuccessful, the coup attempt of October 2, 1977 was bloody and ideologically explosive enough to force zia to ensure his legitimacy by holding a presidential eletion in June, 1978. In elections Zia was elected President for five years providing him legitimate authority to rule. Zia increased his control over the political process and the same time seemed to relinquish some control by establishing a parliament. "All through his rise to power zia tried to optimise his political and military strategies. Sensing that as long as social injustice prevails in

61. Emajuddin Ahamed, Military Rule and the Myth of Democracy, (Dhaka : University Press Ltd. 1988), p. 109.

the larger socioety with spill-over effects on the country's armed forces, which would make it extremely difficult, if not possible, for the concept of political legitimacy to make firm social roots."[62] Zia emphasised for the establishment of democracy expressing that, "true and effective application of democracy and confidence in it are like blessings on the life of the people of any country. Nobody can either or think that the Bangladesh nation shall be deprived of their blessing."[63]

Thus, Ziaur Rehman gave importance for political legitimacy. "For Zia-ur-Rahman, the returen to the pillars of Islam for a basis of the state was a tune worth playing, for it, restored a balance in policy more comfortable for a military man than the Awami league pillars of the state. An Islamic base justified authoritarian behaviour and set aside temporarily at least, the inconvenience of democratic principles and a character of displying them. Consequently muslim leaders who had been accused of collaboration with Pakistan in 1971 were relieved of the threat of legal action against them by the repeal of the collaborators act."[64] "Religious parties were allowed to organise formally in 1976, and muslim festivals were encouraged particularly by the active participation of officials."[65] As

---

62. Zillur R. Khan, Op. cit, p. 560.

63. See Apendix-III for zia's Speech.

64. M. Rashiduzzaman, "Changing Political Patterns in Bangladesh : Internal Constratints and External Fears" in M.M. Khan and H.M. Zaffarullah (eds), Politics and Bureaucracy in New Nation : Bangladesh (Dacca : Centre for Administrative Studies, 1980) p. 185.

65. Ibid.

much as possible was done to mobilise political support among muslims in the armed forces to reinforce martial law administration. "Islam was promoted not for purely religious purposes but as an agency for the extension and preservation of his power, a means rather than an end."[66] Zia's behaviour in this respect fits the instrumentalist mode very well and no where were its benefits more obvious than in the military forces themselves. "Each wing of armed forces was politicised, and the army in particular was riddled with Bangladesh and Islamic identity to the nation zia tried to legitimise his military rule."

A return to islamic principles helped to accomplish a good deal within the army and the state. It also helped to strengthenties with wealthy muslim states, which energised its fluctuating economy by the injections of valuable foreign exchange.

Zia's attempts of islamic polity were in accordance with the francis robinson's Brass thesis" That "Islamic polity exists because an elite can most easily attain and maintain power by mainpulating religion for political purposes."[68]

---

66. Danis Wright, "Islam and Bangladesh Polity," South Asia : Journal of South Asian Studies Vol. X, No. 2 Dec. 1987, p. 22.

67. Lawrence Lifschultz, Bangladesh : The Unfinished Revolution (London : zed Press, 1979). p. 30.

68. Francis Robinson, "Nation-Formation : The Brass Thesis and Muslim Separtism in David Taylor's and Malcolm Yapp's Collection of Essays," Political Identity in south Asia (London : Curzon Press, 1979), p. 79.

Zia's model of checks and balances within the armed forces presented the blue print for republic's military organisation. The blue print was designed to contain the rising expectations of soldiers. The military scheme was not only to dissipate the rival leadership within the army but also to reconstruct the armed forces. Another of Zia's strategies was to make the elected assembly completely dependent upon the armed forces, so as to strengthen the military institution. In this regard zia government's efforts to militarize the government were even more subtle that Ayub's, zia made efforts to civilianse his rule but the real custodians of power continued to be the military. The civil-military bureaucrats continued to play the decisive role. By winning two major elections President Zia succeeded in civilianising his military regime. He announced withdrawal of martial law on April 6, 1979 in order to establish a healthy democratic order which could lead the country towards a happy and prosperous life.[69] But he faced terrible opposition within the army. His moves were considered as steps towards over democratisation of political system.

As Zia hastened his civilianisation process, many in the armed forces began to fear that he might become too powerful and less amenable to military. "Zia's quest for civilian legitimation inevitably distanced him from the armed forces which were averse to sharing a sizeable proportion of the resources to which the state had access. With leading segments of the newly established ruling party (B.N.P.). Underlying the restiveness of the military in the face of this new development were two other major factors-viz. the resentment of the military against the bureaucracy taking off more and more of the surlus, aid money and other resources under the new dispensation and the political consequences of the inter position of a civilian structure of authority in the hinterland, where the military had become accustomed to regarding itself as the direct extension of the state power."[70]

Despite the authoritarian character of Zia's government, the military personnel were not happy with his policies of over democratisation. "What precipitated the fall of Zia and the coup attempt of May 1981 which killed Zia, was the transfer order of Manzoor, who believed that if he brought about Zia's downfall, he might receive necessary support from Dhaka. But his risky venture resulted in his own downfall too. The coup was led by about 20 officers."[71]

"The coups were that result of the conversion of conventional army into a guerrilla force and their its reconversion back into a conventional army."[72] The memebers who were deserted from regular forces and fought guerrilla war during liberation of Bangladesh were politicised and radicalised to a great extent. There were the members of regular armed forces of Bangladesh, who wanted to production oriented institution and sought role into the af-

---

69. See Appendix-IV for Zia's address.

70. T.V. Sathyamurti, "Betrayal of Civilian Politics," Economic and political Weekly, Vol. XX, No. 18, May 4, 1985.

71. Emajuddin Ahamed, Op.cit. p. 114.

72. Takukder Maniruzzamen, Group Interests and Political Changes. Op.cit, p. 252.

fairs of the State. Such moves resulted in factionalism and affected the discipline and loyalty among the rank and file. Thus, "whenever a hero of liberation war felt deprived of something which he thought he deserved, whether it was his lack of voice in the affairs of the nation or denial or a promotion or dismissal from a job he, together with his friends often simply launched a guerrilla type operation designed to liquidate the head of the government and seized power.[73] The coup attempt of 30 May, 1981 like the previous several coup attempts was staged by disgruntled freedom fighters. So, the coup could be accounted mainly to the corporate interests of the army.

The coup attempt was quite significant,[74] firstly, it signalled the end of the influence of the freedom fighter's group in the armed forces. Secondly, this incident paved the way for an integrated and well knit armed forces in Bangladesh. Thirdly, this incident demonstrated clearly that any attempt to seize power from a peripheral zone, without involving those at the centre of power, was bound to fail.

After the assassination of zia, justice Abdus Sattar was sworn in as acting President of Bangladesh and a constitutional government was installed. The interregnum between Zia's assassination and Ershad's proclamation of Martial law can hardly be called a civilian phase free from interference by the army. Justice Sattar the 75 year old successor to Zia was acceptable to armed forces. When he

---

73. Ibid.

74. For detail see, Emajuddin Ahamed op. cit, pp. 116-117.

took over as acting President according to the succession rule provided for, in the Bangladesh Constitution, the chiefs of armed forces took oath of loyalty to the new President.

Thus, army earned reputation of allowing political succession to follow a constitutional route. In fact, it was with the army's support that acting President Sattar was chosen as a B.N.P. candidate, for the Presidential election in November, 1981. It was again with the help of army that he was able to win a massive victory in the elections and became elected President of the country. Sattar expressed his enjoyment of trust and respect of the country's armed forces.[75] At the same time the army wanted to ensure that President Sattar did not go out of its control to establish a civilian regime depriving the army of its share in the decision-making process of the governemt. Such a power sharing mechanism, Ershad argued, ensured the stability of the government. He demanded for the military, a constitutional the government. He demanded for the military, a constitutional role to ensure the protection of the political system, for nation building and for bringing effective democracy.[76] (See Appendix-V). Gen. Ershad said that the late president Zia-ur-Rahman had given an excellent concept, "This concept required us to depart from the conventional Western ideas about the role of the armed forces. It called for combining the tasks of nation building and national defence into one concept of total national defence."[77] he said that the role of armed forces should be reassessed in

75. The Bangladesh Times, November 10, 1981.

76. See Appendix-V for Ershad's views.

77. Bangladesh Times, Nov. 29, 1981.

this new perspective.

In an interview with Peter Nieswand, Gen. Ershad expressed his strong feeling that, "the army should be directly associated with the governance of the country, which might fulfil the ambition of the army and might not lead to further coups."[78] In another interview with an Indian Newsmen at his official residence, Ershad said, "this is necessary to prevent repetition of assassinationof Presidents by the army which 'must be kept happy.' He said candidly that, "the army's role should be institutionalised as Bangladesh was not like India whose leaders were very mature."[79]

But after elections President Sattar was so impressed by his massive victory and so emboldened with the wish to restore democracy and civilian supremacy that he began to assert himself vis-a-vis army. Two days after elections he declared that in a democracy, the army has no further role to play other than safeguarding the national security. This led to a rift between civilian and military administration and a weak Sattar could not stand firm for long against mounting pressures from army for power sharing.

By this time armed forces of Bangladesh had dissolved their mutual differences. They had come closer for two main reasons. Firstly, they wanted to participate ac

---

78. The Hindustan Times, Nov, 22, 1981.

79. Times of India. Nov. 22, 1981.

tively in the socio-econmic upliftment of the society and secondly, they wanted a constitutional role in the politics of the country.

As a result, in January 1982 Sattar conceded the army's demand and formed a National Security Council (NSC) to replace the old National Defence Council. The NSC consisting of three service Chiefs under the chairmanship of President, was to function as a top policy making body giving guidelines to the government on national affairs and the needs of the armed services and to explore ways in which the military could participate in the country's socio-economic development.

The B.N.P. government under Sattar could not keep up its image. It became highly factionalised and when it failed in p erformance i n all spheres the military elite moved swiftly and staged a bloodless coup d etat on 24 March, 1982 and martial law was clamped. Ershad declared,

"I, Lieutenment General Hussian Muhammad Ershad, with the help and mercy of Almighty Allah and blessings of our great patriotic people, do hereby take over and assume all and full powers of the government of the People's Republic of Bangladesh with immediate efect from Wednessday, 24th March, 1982 as Chief Martial Law Administrative of the People's Republic of Bangladesh and do hereby, declare that the whole of Bangladesh shall be under martial law with immediate effect along with assumption of power of Chief Martial Law Administrator. I do hereby assume the full command and control of all the armed forces of Bangladesh."[80]

"While 1975 coup was a sad reminder of the radical young officers taking the law into their own hands, the 1981 coup clearly illustrated that it was difficult for a person to rise to power with sufficient support from the rank and file of the army."

The corporate interest of the military and factionalism has been a motivationg factor making coup attempts in Bangladesh, and the coup d etat of March 24, 1982 too can be adequately accounted for in terms of corporate interests of military. The unifies military sought consititutional role in the affairs of the country. As they got deeply entrenched in the centre of power, they could not afford to be indifferent to the socio-political forces shaping politico-economic decisions at the highest level. The military elite helped justice Sattar continue electoral democracy only after their predominence was secured at the national decision making structure and went along with him as long as they felt that their interests were safe. However, in the failure of civil authorities in socio-economic and political sphere, the military elite decovered elements of uncertainty threatening their corporate interests. Hence, they moved swiftly and staged a bloodless coup d' etat on 24 March, 1982.

Gen. Ershad as head of new military regime tried to justify his takeover by refering to the deteriorated socio-

---

80. From text of the Proclamation of Martial Law.

economic conditions. He said to his countrymen, "the national security, independece and sovereignity was threatened due to social and political indiscipline, unprecedented corruption, devastated economy, administrative stalemate, extreme deterioration of law and order and frightening economic and food crisis."[82]

He tries to expand his military base and appointed military personnel almost everywhere. "The military government was unique in the sense that it was often called "Parliament of Soldiers," Where younger officers participated significantly in policy deliberation with senoor officers and some times initiate policies."[83] As is known that Bangladesh's military has always had a considerable factor of factionalism, the new military regime of Gen. Ershad worked to find out a civil-military format to solve, what Gen. Ershad considered the 'deep-seated politico-military problem' in Bangladesh.[84] Thus, it was in the 1982 that many observers argued that factionalism within military had been visibly reduced and that the military had become more unified to safeguard its institutional interests and played an active role in governing the nation. "Gen. Ershas led a force that had never been so homogenous and

81. R.G. Sawhney, "Bangla Army Seeks New Role," The Tribune, Chandigarh, Oct. 19, 1983.

82. Bangladesh Observer, March 25, 1982.

83. Md. Ataur Rahman, "Bangladesh in 1982 : Beginning of the Second Decade," Asian Survey, Vol. XXIII, No. 2, Feb. 1983, p. 151.

84. S. Kamaluddin, "Changing of the Guard", Far Eastern Economic Review, Vol. DVIII, March 19, 1982, p. 13.

professional. All this was the result of gradual revival of the radical elements from the military, but it was also through the communications and sharing of views among the cross-sections of the officer corps and various hierarchies within the military."[85] Thus the process of institutionalisation in military reduced factionalism to a great extent.

Gen. Ershad headed a 17- member council of ministers under the title Chief Martial Law Administrator (CMLA). Eight members of the cabinet were drawn from the military and retired military officers, including two ex-air vice-martials. Ershad had kept some key ministries including Defence, cabinet, establishment and science and technology for himself.[86] Some key cabinet positions were given to leading bureaucrats and other high officials.

Like Zia, Ershad also made attempts to civilianize his rule in order to legitimise the military regime. Lt. Gen. H.M. Ershad said, "We did not snatch away the responsibility of running the affairs of the state. The people of the country hailed the imposition of martial law. The imposition of martial law was very logical, cogent and natural in the light of prevailing situation at that time. There was no alternative open before the nation by which the country could have been saved from utter destruction."[87] Ershad expressed that his martial law regime was different from

---

85. D. Sen, "Army Shadow Over Bangla," Hindustan Times Jan. 9, 1982.

86. M.D. Ataur Rahman, Bangladesh in 1982 : Beginning of the Second Decade, Op.cit. p. 152.

87. Text from Ershad's interview.

previous martial law regime as it had long term plans. He said, "The present government is determined to bring about a revolutionary change in the country. The government is going to introduce permanent measures so that the people do not suffer as victims of dishonest politics again and again. The present Government is determined to take the country towards pregress by bring about change in the economic and social structure."[88] This martial law, he believed, was in the interest of the masses.

In the process, he adopted various long term and short term policies to improve the socio-economic conditions. These included elimination of corruption, decentralisation of the administrative system, disinvestment of industries to private owners, land reforms and educational changes. To achieve the goals he suspended all the political activies of individuals, groups and political parties. Many officials were suspended on the charges of corruption. Administrative decentralisation was a step towards reorganisation of administrative structure of the country. Under this 'Upillas' were the basic units of administration and the central government administrator was be posted there.

However, this system faced problems. Three general types of difficulties were there[89]-First, the system needed full set of experienced administrators. Secondly, the political differences altered the course of seemingly well conceived policy. Thirdly, there were financial resource

---

88. Ibid, p. 1051.

89. Larry Schroede, "Decentralisation in Rural Bangladesh," Asian Survey Vol. XXV, No. 11, Nov. 1985, pp. 1144-1146.

challenges of resource mobilization and allocations. Ershad continued to solidify his regume through various refrendums for his socio-economic policies and als strengthened his rural base through the rural elites. He formed his own Jatiya Party to legitimise his rule.

The emergence of the political parties and their alliances rose against the atrocities of his government. This led to the awakening of the masses and resulted in demonstrations. hartals, strikes and violence. Closely related to the dynamics of domestic political situation was the downward trend in the state of economic effairs. With the rise of opposition alliances, the country started a journey towards a stable democratic polity. The Jatiya Party of Ershad was becoming weak although all the groups apparently pledged loyalty to him. This can be estimated as "Ershad shiffled his cabinet more than 60 times during his less than nine years in office."[90] Ershad was oftern reported as dismayed at the lack of organisational abilities among his associates. Ministers were assigned to look after districts as well as their ministries, but there complaints against them that they spent much more time in Dhaka, than in performing or nurturing the tasks needed to produce the votes necessary to continue Ershad and the J.P. in office. The lack of organisation may be seen in the unspectacular showing of the J.P. in the Up-Zilla elections. Through out 1989 and 1990, there were demonstrations against Ershad. But these were never taken serious. Only once in November, 1987 had rioting taken place on such a

---

90. Craig Baxter, "Bangladesh in 1990 : A New Beginnng," Asian Surver, Vol. XXXI, No. 2, Feb. 1991, p. 147.

scale that it was necessary, in Ershad,s view to declare a state of emergency. But the opposition did not stop by this and the mass upsurge of November, December 1990 resulted in the removal of Ershad from the saddle of power.

Ershad's policy was the one which is often adopted by dominant leaders, that was to shift close associates quickly so that none would retain a position of considerable power long enough to consolidate that power into a competing centre. Perhaps this was the policy which did not allow any other leader to grow to such an extent so as to result in another coup.

During Ershad's regime the military in the country became a wellknit organisation. It became a disciplined organisation under a single command structure. Ideologically, military had faith in Islamic ideals of Ershad. Ershad played his cards quite astutely. "Although he never took recourse to secularism as a political ideology, he did not go out of the way either to project himself as a vocifarous champion of the Islamic ideology, his Pro-Islamic gestures not withstanding. In short, his equivocal stand with regard to the dichotomy between Bengali oriented and Islam oriented Bangladesh nationalism gave him a mixed image which he made reasonably good use of."[91]

There was considerable increase in the official defence allocations, which after two years of Ershad regime was Tk 973 crores. The invisible allocation Tk. 557 crore,

---

91. Partha S. Ghosh, "Bangladesh Politics : Many Imponderables," Mainstream, Vol. XXIX, No. 8 Dec. 15, 1990, p. 6.

the budget allocation were 14% more than the previous year. All this led to the expansion of armed forces and the mushroom growth of its institutions.[92]

Ershad paid a great attention for the material well being of the military officers in terms of promotion avenues, better housing, better rationing, salary hikes and so on. "Following the 1985 referendum which overhelmingly approved Ershad's continuation in power and subsequently following the 1986 parliamentay elections which returned his Jatiya Party as the majority party in parliament, Ershad went ahead with his strategy of pampering the army."[93] According to information available from proceding of Bangladesh Parliament held in early 1987, "53 Posts of superintendent of police (SP) out of a total of 64 went army personnel. 1500 army officers were posted on civilian duties; 97 army officers were appointeed to extremely high ranking civilian posts and so on. In may, 1987, Ershad went to the extent of providing for a representative of the military in each district council through his controversial District Council Ordinance.[94] He, however, could not implement it as it evolved violent protests inspite of the fact that the parliament had approved it. So, leke zia-ur-Rahman Ershad's policy of civilizing the rule by his

---

92. Manash Ghosh, "Bangladesh Today-II : Is the Army Indispensable," The Statesment, Jan. 16, 1984. p. 5.

93. Partha S. Ghosh, "Bangladesh Politics : Many Imponderables", op.cit. p. 3.

94. Ibid.

henchmen of Jatiya Party was only an instrument of avoiding legitimacy crisis.

Table-4

Defence expenditure of Bangladesh in 1973-88:[95]

Year	Defence Expenditure (in million Taks)	Defence expenditure as a % G.D.P.
1973	312	0.5
1974	566	0.6
1975	911	0.8
1976	1408	1.3
1977	1917	1.2
1978	2038	1.1
1979	2409	1.3
1980	2985	1.4
1981	3210	1.3
1982	4190	1.5
1983	5080	1.6
1984	5325	1.4
1985	5796	1.3
1986	7495	1.5
1987	9080	-
1988	10000	-

Convention : - Information not available.

95. World Armaments and Disarmaments, SIPRI, Year Bood, (Cambridge and M/s : The MIT Press, 1974 to 1989.)

The size of Banlgadesh armed forces increased considerably. In an account the growth of Bangladesh increased by 114 percent and its expenditure by 186 percent during 1973 to 1990.[96]

Data in table-4 prove that defence expenditure of Bangladesh was less during civilian regime of Mujib and a brief period of Zia but increased tremendously during the military rules.

Table-5

Number of Armed Forces:[97]

Year	Total number of Regular Forces	Army	Navy	Airforce	Paramilitary forces
1975	26,500	25,000	500	1,000	16000 N.D.F. & 13000 B.D.R.
1980-81	72,000	65,000	4,000	3,000	3000 B.D.R.& 36000 Armed Police reserved
1991-92	106,500	93,000	7,500	6,000	30000 B.B.D.R. Armed Police 500 Ansars Securityguards 20000

96. Dilara Choudhury, op.cit. p. 88.

97. Military Balance (London : 1974-75, 1981-82 and 1990-91.)

Ershad's continued efforts to secure support of the armed forces resulted in his failure to establish his hegemony and domination over the civil society of Bangladesh. As a result Ershad faced many problems from the civil society. Students and civilian political organisations gained strength. Under the repressive measures applied by Ershad the political parties and students organisations gained even more momentum. Several strikes and demonstrations were held. The socio-economic conditions were also not good. Unrest prevailed in the society. As a result of mass upheaval of 1990 Ershad had to resign.

Defence Expenditure:[98]

Year	Tk.	$ M.
1975	470 m	65
1980	2.5 bn.	153
1990	11.30 bn.	326.90

Ershad during his regime did not allow any other military officers to become so strong who could challenge his position. Hence, after his resignation, there was no such leader in the army. Political parties had joined their hands to remove him from his position.

Moreover, at this stage the most critical factor was

98. Ibid.

the attitude of the officers of the armed forces. By now, the officers had come to think that the army as an institution was greater than any individual or political party. The political party of Ershad, Jatiya Party was viewed as being a liability for the army. The army, thus, decided than to hand over power to the Chief Justice of the Supreme Court, Justice Shahabuddin Ahmed. He was given mandate to hold free and fair elections. After the Feb. 27, 1991 election, Civil society prevailed over the armed sector of the state. The armed forces of Bangladesh at this stage could be called as professionalised forces, who seen to have realised that political sphere was not for them.

Bangladesh Army has a total strength of 120,000 personnel organised into seven infantry divisions, one armoured brigade, one artillery division, one air-defence brigade and an engineer brigade. Combat equipment and military hard ware are predominantly of Chinese origin.

Bangladesh Navy has a strength of 10,500 personnel manning four frigates and 45 patrol and coastal combatants. Naval bases are located at Chittagong (HQ), Dhaka. Khulna and Kaptai. All naval combatant crafts stand supplied by China (PRC).

Bangladesh Air Force has 65 combat aircraft (all Chinese fighters manned by a strength of 6500.)

Para-military forces comprise:

-Bangladesh Rifles (border security). Has a strength of 30,000 organised in 41 battalions.

-Ansars (security guards). Has a strength of 20,000 organised into battalions. A further 180,000 are on the rolls as unembodied personnel.

In terms of border security commitments the above forces are required to defend.[99]

-India-Bangladesh border-4023 km

-Myanmar-Bangladesh border-283 km

-Bay of Bengal coastline 580 km.

The Bangladesh Army, like the Pakistan Army is totally dependant on Chinese military hardware. Despite initial opposition to the creation of Bangladesh, the Chinese relented and soon converted Bangladesh into a Chinese military equipment client state. India, in the Chinese context has to note that a very slender strip of 90 km of Indian territory separates Bangladesh from Chinese controlled Tibet.

Some of the Mein features of Bangladesh Armed Forces are:

"*Bangladesh Armed Forces including Bangladesh Rifles came into existence only after 1971. They were not bequeathed by the British to the successor states of India and Pakistan.

*Initial manpower was found from the repatriated Bengali Personnel of the Pakistan Army (East Bengal Regiments) and freedom fighters of the Mukti Bahini.

*The top bierarchy of Bangladesh till recently could be said to be composed of officers who had served in the

99. Dr. Subhash Kapile, 'Bangladesh Armed Forces and Islamic Fundementalism, "South Asia Analysis Group" May,2001.

Pakistan Army during Field Marshal Ayub Khan's regime. Their formative years were conditioned by the inperatives and system of military rule in Pakistan.

*According to one estimate, most of the 400 officers of the rank of Major and above belong to repatriated cadres from the Pakistan Army and find military rule comfortable.

*in terms of socio-economic composition the bulk of the rank and file seem to be drawn from the poor and economically backward rural areas. Therefore, they are suseeptible to Islamic fundamentalist influences that hold sway in such areas.

*In terms of traditions and identity the Bangladesh Armed Forces can be said to follow the Pakistan Army i.e. in the absence of any other roots, to draw on the Islamic heritage and current day trends of Pan Islamism in the Muslim world.

*Like the Pakistan Army the Bangladesh Armed Forces share the following characteristics:

-Perceive itself as the only force holding Bangladesh together.

-Has a poor opinion of Bangladesh's fractious polity and their competence for governance.

-In their perceived mission to hold the country together and putting an end to misgovernance, they have carried out military coups, counter coups and even assassination of military Presidents.

-Should have a say in the country's foreign policy."

In the leck of the evolution of enough political democratic institutions in Bangladesh and multifaceted socio-economic problems military establishments seem to be tired of stepping into the political spheres as peace keepers. The situations where it is easy and they can find enough reasons to step into the politics, they seem to refrain from such indulgences. Or to say that professionalism is creeping into the Bangladesh military spheres and now it is turn to develop or raise political institutions to the levels to keep and hold power for long. Another reason for military to refrain from indulgences or to be passive can be that just as in political scene, in military too there is leadership crises.

As far as the masses are concerned they want peace, stability, civil order with corruption wiped out, from that do not seem to mind even military interventions as far as they instill confidence ion people.

However after establishing and backing interim government in Bangladesh recently and sending the former prime minister to exile under corruption charges, Farid Ahmed remarks, "An army backed plan to marginalize country's main political parties and their leaders may result in serious damage to the democratic fabric of the country"100

Military backed government may form new political parties. Military chief general, Moeen recently in a meeting with editors of the dailies told that neither he nor Bangladesh army has any interntion to take over the charge of the government and to run it. They are playing a supporting role to this civil administration run by Dr. Fakhruddin Ali Ahmed.

Army came to scene on January 11, 2007 when emergency rule was declaed and people were relieved from the

---

100. Farid Ahmed, Bangladesh : Army Backed Reforms Imperil Democracy, IPS july 19, 2007.

axphyziated political environmentand inevitable civil war after the declaration of election on January 22, 2007. Gen Moeen lauded the positive role of the army in an effort to establish 'New Democracy' The speculation of confused masses became clear, that new political parties can be launched to replace the caretaker government in the time to come. Thus, the military establishments have acted almost in the manner the way it has been doing in the past.

From the military establishement in Bangladesh, it is clear that its politicised character leads it into the political sphere. The autonomious structural composition, the recruitment policies, training, skill-structure and low level of professionalisation helped military to step into the political sphere. Military's power within the country was result of both its command over the means of violence and its willingness to use them politically. The military organisation also affected the military's orientation towards politics. Military's prestige and honour lead it into the politics but factionalism in military due to ideological differences and personal ambitions of militry personnel led to coups and counter-coups. This indiscipline in military worked to pull down the image of military.

However, in a democratically weak political system of a country like Bangladesh, military officers can walk the corridors of power any time, they want. Therefore, unless the military chooses to remove itself from the body politic of the country in the long term interest of its people and their security, there is nothing the people of Bangladesh can do about it. The military is, thus, the final arbiter of the destiny of Bangladesh.

VII-Summary of Findings

The role of military in the politics is a complex and dynamic phenomenon. Soon after their independence, most of the Afro-Asian countries were plagued by recurring military interventions in the politics thwarting democratic process in the bud itself. Therefore, a humble effort has been made in this thesis to find out the causes of military intervention in politics in general and in Bangladesh in particular. An effort has been made ot link mocro study, so that, a contribution to develop oa general theory of role of military in politics can be made. The role of military in politics is quite different in the developed countries than in the underdeveloped countries. The military in developing countries percieves its role only to defend the country from external aggression but also takes pride in the task of nation-building.

Most of the studies available on the problem are unidimensional. The scholars attributed the problem either to enironment or to the nature of military establishment. In fact, the problem is multidimensional, an amalgam of environmental conditions as well as military establishment variables. Environmental conditions not only include the polity, economy and society but history is also an important factor. The objectivity of the problem has to be made conscious by subjective orientation of the nature of military establishment. When military becomes c onscious about the objective conditions, only then, it steps into the environmental arena. Main environmental variables which affect military's r ole in p olitics are low institutionalisation, high mobilisation, low political culture, lack of democratic institutions, absence of effective, well organised political parties and pressure groups, poor socioeconomic conditions, cleavaged society, identity problem, leadership crisis, legitimacy crisis, political unrest and rampant corruption, The environment of Bangladesh and the nature of military both are conducive for military's intervention in politics.

The role of military in Bangladesh is related to the general experience of the developing countries. Like other developing countries, in Bangladesh also, the Westernerspectives were superimposed on its society after gaining independence, which viewed capitalist development as the only desirable path and believed that it was the final stage of development. Under this approch, the administrative apparatus not only remained a concrete form of state power but also occupied considerable political space. And the increasing dependency on the coercive organs like, police, para-military and military resulted in wide ranging crisis in the society. The use of force without a development ideology in poverty ridden society resulted in legitimacy crisis. It created a situation where different sections of society resorted to aggressive destroyed the existing structure, but could not offer an alternative. Such crisis of legitimacy led to up-root the democracy from the society and sowed the seeds of authoritarian government.

Bangladesh came into existence after a long independence movement, which was a reaction against the colonial masters of West Pakistan. The creation of Bangladesh suggested that only the Islamic factor which was common in East and West Pakistan, on which Pakistan got separated from India was not an effective force to keep them united.

Thus, Bangladesh developed identity problem since its inception. In Bangladesh liberation war erstwhile Bengali army played important role along with political and armed guerrilla groups. Therefore, army was politicised since its independence. The participation of military along with the political groups in the liberation war, provided for the historical peculiarity and contedtuality for the politicisation of Bangladesh army. Moreover, Awami league had no political ideology or policies for future socio-economic development. They just wanted a separate autonomious state and the whole polity revolved round one leader, Sheikh Mujibur Rahman. Hence, the lack of policy crientation and plurality of leadership, later resulted into socio-political, socio-economic and leadership crisis, enough to induce military to come into political spheres of the country.

After independence, although Mujib adopted parliamentary democracy but under defective apparatus of Awami League (which had various factions, each with selfish interests) he could not handle the post-independence period according to democratic norms. And this created a sense of dissatisfaction among the masses. This dissatisfaction and frustraction of the army personnel resulted in his brutal killing. This created vacuum in political sphere, as there was no other mass based political party and/or alternative leadership, which could guide the country towards the democratic path. In such situations the democracy could not take the roots in the country and due to lack of democratic institutions started crumbling. Such environment had the positive potential for military to play its role actively in political sphere as the crisis of legitimacy had left the civilian government impotent, in the face of growing instability and growing frustration against the social order. Sheikh Mujib himself sounded deathknell to the democracy by abondoning conpetetive multi-party system and replacing it by one party rule of B.A.K.S.A.L. His IVth amendment of the constitution, by which he became almost a dictator, later, paved an easy way for the military into the political sphere. By developing and favouring J.R.B., a personal institution within the military, he had already discarded the norm of military neutrality.

Bangladesh's military had been operating in an environment in which the level of public attachment to civilian institutions was very low. Civilian institutions were not recognised as being a complex of procedures and organs recognised by a broad consensus in society as duty worthy. Mass based political parties and civilian pressure groups. such as trade unions were few and far between, the procedure for transfer of power by election or by any other method was irregular, almost non existent and the location of supreme authority, a matter of acute disagreement.

Under the prevailing conditions of corruption, break down of law and order and political instability, military was the only instituion which emerged, which had charismatic reputation. It was viewed as the only institution which could fill the institutional void in the political system of Bangladesh.

The environmental socio-economic conditions, low political institutionalisation, along with low political culture are thus the important determiners of the entry of military in the arena of politics. However, it is not the environment alone but also the nature and organisation of the military itself which induced it to enter the political sphere. The environmental conditions are like catalytic agents; it is the nature of military establishment which brings the componental changes in the society.

The Bangladesh army had the past legacy for its political role, first inherited from Britishers and then from Pakistan. It had the experience under the military regimes of Ayub and Yahaya, Such a politicised army when fought for the liberation of the country, harboured some ambitions of having some represetation in the political affairs of the country after liberation. Also, various armed groups which had taken arms for the liberation of the country were not politically neutral. The frequent use of the armed forces on the disturbed areas under social crisis i.e. 'aid to civil' further helped these forces to develop political outlook. They developed nationalistic ideology. Along with all this, their skills and technical advancement helped them to come into the sphere of politics. However, it is to be noted that unlike Pakistani army, the Bangladeshi army had many factions in it, it was not a cohesive group. Hence, the factionalism in the armed forces resulted in coups and counter coups. Army was first divided on the basis of pro-India and pro-Pakistani loyality and later on, on the basis of ideology and personal loyality. It had mainly three different groups : rightists, who believed in Bangladesh ideology; Mujibists, who believed in the principles of nationalism, secularism, socialism and democracy; leftists, who believed in the class-less and socialistic ideogy.

Once they came into power, they showed reluctance to go back to their barracks and did not allow the democratic traditions to take roots. After the assassination of zia, Ershad did not allow the elected representative of the state to remain in power and took control over it, proving that an intervention breeds the germs of another such intervention and that even if a popularly elected civilian governement comes to power and tries to circumscribe its roles, there is strong resistence to such initiative.

The performance of successive military regimes under zia and Ershad produced mixed results. Gen. Zia's regime in Bangladesh contributed substantially to restoring multiparty democracy and made some grogress in economic matters as well by liberalising the economy. By building national and local level institutions, an attempt was also made for political participation of masses. The Bangladesh National Party, he created, had also championed the cntinuity of democratic institutions and argued for maintenance of presidency as a living institution. of President zia, the founder of party, more skillfully than its predecessor, the Awami League. The Awami League transformed a multiparty parliamentary form of government into one party presidential type, where as the B.N.P. transformed a martial law administration into a civilian government through electoral means and directed the nation towards peace and stability under democratic norms. The valuable contribution of Gen. Zia and his B.N.P. towards military's withdrawal from politics and restoration of democracy was, however, negated through the strong arm dictates of Gen. Ershad, who had taken the reins of government in his own hands. Gen. Ershad destroyed all the political institutions and did not try to give a mass base to his Jatiya Party, thus leaving the progress actually achieved in some sectors of economy by its leberalisation, as meaningless. Successive military governments in Bangladesh devoted much attention to industrial activities, road construction and urban development programme, since these represented interests of urban middle classes and thus helped in expanding their own support base. Military ruler's civilianisation process was thus, nothing but a strategic legitimisation of their rules.

Military came in the political sphere to ensure national development as a modernizing instrument for bringing rapid socio-economic development by building effective democratic political institutions in the traditional and transitional society of Bangladesh. But, the military rules only served to strengthen the praetorian tradition in Bangladesh. Like most military regimes, the military regimes of Bangladesh also favoured the status-quo. Any attempt to radicalise the socio-economic order was met with by the military officers by force. Military proved itself incapable of dealing with the more elusive problems of development. They ware seen preoccupied with their own class interests and were described so antipolitical as to frustrate their efforts to gain popular support. Military rulers, repeatedly demonstrated their low political bargaining and economic management capabilities. Their performance in political institution building was found dismal and negative. Moreover, their role expansion in the day to day, politico-administrative affairs not only impaired their military skills, but also their distinctive professional values and hightened the repeated military interventions.

The full analysis of the performance of military regimes in Bangladesh reveals that there was not much improvement in the deteriorated socio-economic conditions and in the low political institutionalisation of the country, except for a brief period of Zia's civilianisation process when he accelerated the process of socio-economic modernisation and institutionalisation. Aggregate analysis thus establishes that even the military regimes performed no better than civilian regime. Whatever may be the performance of military regimes, it is, however clear that the deteriorated environmental conditions are the factors which grease the path for military's political actions.

The military establishment factors also have a tendency for military's political role. Three main factors appear to link the military to the state in Bangladesh. They are identity, colonial and structural linkages. Inspite of the great factionalism, the Bangladesh army has effective autonomous organisation. It is homogenous ethnically, linguistically and religiously but highly heterogenous, ideologically. It played heroic role in Bangladesh liberation war and got politicised but, the politicisation was actually a colonial ligacy. Religion plays an important role in forming structural linkages. Historically, Islam has had a special relationship with the Muslim Armies. Indentification with Islam reinforced the military's commitment to the state. The religion has been a powerful motivating force for the Bangladesh army. political actions by the military in 1975 to 1981 show that the Military's allegiance to the state and religion took precedent over that to the government in power. It is apparent that when Islamic fundamentalism is promoted as a state ideology, it is incompatiable with the modernisation and democractisation of a society. Military governments need ideology to legitimise their rule and ensure their stability.

Whenever military government comes to power it tries to wipe out corruption by punishing politicians and civil servants. It is easier for the military to do this, people appreciate this but they don't support military for long time because of its autocratic tendencies. Moreover, military rule does not and cannot improve the socio-economic conditions better than the civilian rule. Like civilian regimes military also tries to legitimise its rule by building popular political institutions in order to incorporate the interests of both military and civilian groups. But the ever rising era of high expections of people cause frustration among masses and they frequently opt for changes in political leaderships. In a society like Bangladesh, when political leadership mostly remained in the hands of military leaders, the changes in polity or political leadership meant changes in military leadership. These changes in military leadership occured generally through coups and counter-coups either blooded or bloodless.

Even if the government adopts a civilian rule in which the military becomes constitutionally subordinate to the government, the potential for military intervention would remain until the military becomes highly professionalised and itself parts with its political functions. however, the new recruits of Bangladesh armed forces have no experience of the liberation war and they consider politics as a 'dirty game' hence, they are not politically oriented. They are more progressive and more democratic in their out look. Apparently, their motivation is more careerist and professional than their highly politicised senior officers. The new generation are the future leaders of the army. Moreover, recent developments reveal that the army is relatively more united than before, it shows that Bangladesh will soon have a small, unified, strong and professional armed force. Along with the professional armed forces, political stability and healthy environmental conditions are must or smooth functioning of a democratic polity.

However, it can not be assumed that the decline and defeat of authoritarian regimes and their replacement by democratic politics necessarily means that democracy will survive in a society. The process of consolidation and strengthening of democracy is a complicated and riskly process. It demands a higher level of rationality on the part of both policy makers and implementers. It also requires changes in the political cultures, political institutions and fundamentally in the adoption of the elite class to the new situations and requirements. All these measures should be taken against prevailing economic difficulties and growing social expections and demands in order to avoid the role of military in the politics of Bangladesh.

The opportunistic politics have degenerated the democratic process in Bangladesh. This has AL and BNP on one side and Islamic, leftist and military on the other. There is no sign of immediate new leadership.

The experimentations with establishing of democracy is still continuing even after thirty-six year of Independence, Bangladesh is still standing at the crossroads of a democratic civilian governments and military rule.

Amidst the continuing political crises what remains to be seen is, whether Bangladesh will allow its citizens to exercise their right to vote under free and fair electoral system which the opposition has been demanding. In turn this will also prove whether Bangladesh wants to strengthen the roots of democracy or moves away from it.

The endless debates, distress and factionalism in the politics and inadequate growth of institutions along with the legitimacy crises have time and again perpetuated a situations for political unrest and instability. The question which instantly hits thc mind is : Is it inevitable for Bangladesh to come out of the vicious circle of political turmoils?

Bibliography

Reports

Bangladesh, country report, The Economist Intelligence Unit, (London, 1993)

Bangladesh Documents, (Madras : The B.N.K.C. Press, 1971).

Bids Research Report, No. 5, (Dhaka, 1988).

Encyclopaedia of Third World, Vol. I, (London : Mansell Publishing Ltd. 1992).

Government of People's Republic of Bangladesh, Ministry of Information and Broadcasting, Department of Publication, Bangladesh Progress, The First Five Year Plan 1973-1978, (Dhaka, 1973).

How Pakistan Violated Human Rights in Bangladesh (Issued Under the Auspices of World Affairs, New Delhi, 1972).

International Conference on Bangladesh, 221, 223, Rouse Avenue, New Delhi, 1971.

K. Subrahamanyam, Military Aid to Pakistan and its Repurcussions on Bangladesh in International Conference on Bangladesh, I.D.S.A. (New Delhi, 1972).

Public Opinion Trends (POT), Analysis and News Services, Bangladesh series, (New Delhi, 1975-1993).

Statistic Abstracts of Bangladesh, Economic Research

Bureau, Socom (Calcutta : Society and Commerce Publication, 1972).

Statistical Bulletin of Bangladesh, 1993, Bureau of Statistics, Ministry of Planning, Government of People's Republic of Bangladesh, (Dhaka, 1993).

Statistical Digest of Bangladesh, Bangladesh Bureau of Statistics, Government of People's Republic of Bangladesh (Dhaka, 1972).

Statistical Pocket Book of Bangladesh, Bangladesh Bureau of Statistics, Ministry of Planning, Government of People's Republic of Bangladesh, (Dhaka, 1992).

The Constitution of People's Republic of Bangladesh, Passed by Constituent Assembly of Bangladesh, (Dhaka, November 4, 1972).

The Military Balance, (London : 1974-75 to 1991-92).

Whitaker's Almaneck, 1993, (London : Whitaker & Sons Ltd. 1993).

World Armament and Disarmamen, SIPRI Year Book, (Cambridge, 1971 to 1988).

World Bank's Annual Report, 1978, (Washington, D.C. 1978).

World Development Report, 1991, The Challenge of Development, World Development Indicators, (New Yourk : Oxford University Press, May 31, 1991).

World Military Expenditure and Arms Transfers U.S. Armed Control and Disarmament Agency (Washington : D.C. 1985, 1987, 1989).

Books :

Abrahamsson, Bengt; Military Professionalisitation

and political Power (London : Sage Publication, 1972).

Ahamed, Emajuddin; Military Rule and The Myth of Democracy (Dhaka : University Press Ltd., 1988)

Ahmad, Borhanuddin; The Generals of Pakistan and Bangladesh, (New Delhi : Vikas Publishing House Pvt. Ltd, 1993).

Ahmad, Kabiruddin, Breakup of Pakistan : Background and Prospects of Bangladesh (London, 1972).

Ahmad, Zakaria Haji and Gouch, Harold; Military Civilian Relations in South-East Asia (Singapore : Oxford University Press, 1985).

Ahmed, Moudud; Bangladesh : Constitutional Quest for Autonomy. Bangladesh 1950-1971 (Bangladesh : University Press Ltd. 1979).

Ahmed, Moudud; Era of Sheikh Mujibur Rahman (Bangladesh : University Press Ltd. 1983).

Ahmed, Rafiuddin (ed); Religion Nationalism and Politics in Bangladesh (New Delhi : South Asian Publishers, 1990).

Ahmed, Sharifuddin; Dacca (London : Curzon Press, 1986).

Akhtar, jamnadas; The Saga of Bangladesh (Delhi : Oriental Publishers, 1971).

Ali, S.M; After the Dark Night (Delhi : Thomson Press India Ltd. 1973).

Ali, Tariq; Pakistan : Military Rule or People's Power (New York : William Morrow & Company, 1970).

Andreski, Stanislav; Military Organization and Society, (Berkley : 1968).

Apter, David; The Politics of Modernization (Chicago : the University of Chicago Press, 1965).

Ayoob, Mohammad and Subrahmayam K; The Liberation War, (New Delhi : S. chand & Co. Pvt. Ltd. 1972).

Bahadur, Kalim; and Singh, Uma (ed); Pakistan : Transition to D emocracy (New Delhi : Patriot Publishers, 1989).

Bahadur, Kalim; Chopra V. Dand Haksar, P.N. (eds); South Asia in Transition : Conflicts and Tensions (New Delhi : Patriot Publishers, 1986).

Balough, Andras and Iman, Zafar; A Political History of National Liberation Movement in Asia and Africa (New Delhi : A.B.C. Publishing House, 1988).

Banerjee, D.N., East Pakistan : A Case Study in Muslim Politics Delhi : Vikas Publications, 1969).

Banerjee, Subrata; Bangladesh (New Delhi : National Book Trust, 1981).

Basu, Gautham Kumar; The State Development and Military Interventions (New Delhi : South Publishers Pvt. Ltd. 1991).

Baxter, Craig; Bangladesh : A new Nation in an Old Setting (Boulder : Colo Westview, 1984).

Baxter, Craig; Malik. K : Yogendra; Kenney, Charles H, and Obert, Robert C.; Government and Politics in South Asia (London : Westview Press, 1987).

Bhatnagar, Yatrindra; Mujib : The Arichitect of Bangladesh (An ISSD) Indian School Supply. Dept Publication, 1971.

Bhattacharjee; Dateline Mujibnagar (Delhi : Vikas Publishing House Pvt. Ltd. 1973).

Bienen, Henry (ed.); The Military Intervenes : Case Studies in Development (New York : Russel Sage Foundation, 1968).

Blackburn, Robin (ed.); Explosion in the Sub-continent India. Pakistan, Bangladesh and Cylone. (Hammods.

1975).

Boyer, William W; A Report on Development Administration in Bangladesh (Dacca : Asia Foundation, April, 1975), Typed Script.

Bunltjens, Ralph; The Decline of Democracy (Orbis Book Aseria, 1978).

Chakrabarty, S.K; The Evolution of Politics in Bangladesh : 1947-78, (New Delhi : Associated Publishing House, 1978).

Chakravarty, S.R. and Narain, Virendra (eds.); Bangladesh : History and Culture (New Delhi : South Asian Publishers, 1986).

Chakravarty, S.R; Bangladesh : Democratic Power (New Delhi : South Asian Publishers, 1986).

Chakravarty, S.R. ; Bangladesh : The Ninteen Seventy Elections (New Delhi : South Asian Publishers, 1987).

Chandra, Probodh; Bloodbath in Bangladesh (New Delhi : Adarsh Publications, 1971).

Chawla, Sudrshan and Sardesai, D.R. (eds.); Changing Patterns of Security in Asia (New York : Praeger Publishers, 1980).

Chopra, Pran; India's Second Liberation (Delhi : Vikas Publishing House, 1973).

Clapham, Cristopher and Philp, George (ed.); The Political Dilemmas of Military Regimes (London : Groom Helm Ltd. 1985).

Cohen, Stephen P; Arms and Politics in Bangladesh (Buffalo Council on International Affairs, 1973).

Das Gupta, R.K; Revolt in East Bengal (Delhi : Navana Printing Works Pvt. Ltd. 197[illegible]).

Decalo, Samuel; Coups and Role : Studies in Military Style (New Haven : Yale University Press, 1976).

Denitch, Bogdan; Legitimation of Regimes, (London : Sage Publications, 1979).

Dennis, Peter; and Parston, Adrian (eds.); Soldiers and Statseman (London : Croom Helm, 1976).

Diamond, Larry, Ling and Lipset (eds.); Democracy in Asia (New Delhi : Vistaar Publiciations, 1989).

Dolgopolov, Yevgeny; The Army and the Revolutionary Transformation of Society (Moscow : Progress Publications, 1981).

Donell, Charles Peter O; Bangladesh : Biography of a Muslim Nation (London : Westview Press, 1984).

Donnell, Guillermo O; Schmitter, Philippe C; and Whitehead, Laurence (eds.); Transitions from Authoritarian Rule : Prospects for Democracy (Baltimore : The Johns Hoppins, University Press, 1987).

Doorn Jacques Van (ed.); Armed Forces and Society (The Hague : Mouton, 1968).

Doorn, Jacques Van (ed.); Military Profession and Military Regime (Hague : Mounton & Co. 1969).

Emerson, Rupert; From Empire to Nation (Boston : Beacon Press, 1963).

Etienne, Gilbert; Bangladesh Development in Perspective (Delhi : The Macmillan Company of India Ltd. 1979).

Faaland, J and Parkinson, J.K.; Bangladesh : The Test Case of Development (New Delhi, 1977).

Falcon and Papanek (eds.); Development Policy : The Pakistan Experience (London : Harvard University Press, 1971).

Feldman, Herbert; Evolution in Pakistan : A study of the Martial Law Administration (London : Oxford University Press, 1967).

Finer, Samuel E; The Man on Horseback : The Role of the Military in Politics (Harmondsworth : Penguin Books, 1975).

Gardezi, Hasan; and Rasid, Jamil (eds.) Pakistan : The Roots of Dictatorship : The Political Economy of a Praetorian State (Delhi : Oxford University Press, 1983).

Gary, Capt, S.K; Spotlight : Freedom Fighters of Bangladesh (New Delhi : Allied Publishers Pvt. Ltd. 1984).

Geertz, Clifford (eds.); Old Societies and New States (New York : The Free Press of Glencoe, 1963).

Goodnow, Henry, F; The Civil Service of Pakistan (New Haven : 1964).

Gough, Kathleen and Sharma, H.P. (ed.); Imperialism and Revolution in South Asia (New York : Monthly Review Press, 1973).

